THE LUCENT LIBRARY OF SCIENCE AND TECHNOLOGY

Black Holes

by Don Nardo

LUCENT
BOOKS®

THOMSON

GALE

San Diego • Detroit • New York • San Francisco • Cleveland • New Haven, Conn. • Waterville, Maine • London • Munich

THOMSON
———★———™
GALE

On cover: Of the three bright dots in the middle of this photo of the center of our galaxy, the one on the left, known as Sagittarius A*, is thought to be a supermassive black hole.

LIBRARY OF CONGRESS CATALOGING-IN-PUBLICATION DATA

Nardo, Don, 1947–
   Black holes / by Don Nardo.
      p. cm. — (The Lucent library of science and technology)
   Summary: Discusses the history and current state of scientific understanding of black holes, exploring what they are, how they are formed, potential uses, and what they tell us about the fate of the universe.
   Includes bibliographical references.
   ISBN 1-59018-101-8 (alk. paper)
   1. Black holes (Astronomy)—Juvenile literature. [1. Black holes (Astronomy)] I. Title. II. Series.
   QB843.B55N37 2004
   523.8'875—dc22
                                                                 2003015069

Printed in the United States of America

Table of Contents

Foreword

"The world has changed far more in the past 100 years than in any other century in history. The reason is not political or economic, but technological—technologies that flowed directly from advances in basic science."

— Stephen Hawking, "A Brief History of Relativity," *Time,* 2000

The twentieth-century scientific and technological revolution that British physicist Stephen Hawking describes in the above quote has transformed virtually every aspect of human life at an unprecedented pace. Inventions unimaginable a century ago have not only become commonplace but are now considered necessities of daily life. As science historian James Burke writes, "We live surrounded by objects and systems that we take for granted, but which profoundly affect the way we behave, think, work, play, and in general conduct our lives."

For example, in just one hundred years, transportation systems have dramatically changed. In 1900 the first gasoline-powered motorcar had just been introduced, and only 144 miles of U.S. roads were hard-surfaced. Horse-drawn trolleys still filled the streets of American cities. The airplane had yet to be invented. Today 217 million vehicles speed along 4 million miles of U.S. roads. Humans have flown to the moon and commercial aircraft are capable of transporting passengers across the Atlantic Ocean in less than three hours.

The transformation of communications has been just as dramatic. In 1900 most Americans lived and worked on farms without electricity or mail delivery. Few people had ever heard a radio or spoken on a telephone. A hundred years later, 98 percent of American homes have telephones and televisions and more than 50 percent have personal computers. Some families even have more than one television and computer, and cell phones are now commonplace, even among the young. Data beamed from communication satellites routinely predict global weather conditions and fiber-optic cable, e-mail, and the Internet have made worldwide telecommunication instantaneous.

Perhaps the most striking measure of scientific and technological change can be seen in medicine and public health. At the beginning of the twentieth century, the average American life span was forty-seven years. By the end of the century the average life span was approaching eighty years, thanks to advances in medicine including the development of vaccines and antibiotics, the discovery of powerful diagnostic tools such as X rays, the life-saving technology of cardiac and neonatal care, and improvements in nutrition and the control of infectious disease.

Rapid change is likely to continue throughout the twenty-first century as science reveals more about physical and biological processes such as global warming, viral replication, and electrical conductivity, and as people apply that new knowledge to personal decisions and government policy. Already, for example, an international treaty calls for immediate reductions in industrial and automobile emissions in response to studies that show a potentially dangerous rise in global temperatures is caused by human activity. Taking an active role in determining the direction of future changes depends on education; people must understand the possible uses of scientific research and the effects of the technology that surrounds them.

The Lucent Books Library of Science and Technology profiles key innovations and discoveries that have transformed the modern world. Each title strives to make a complex scientific discovery, technology, or phenomenon understandable and relevant to the reader. Because scientific discovery is rarely straightforward, each title explains the dead ends, fortunate accidents, and basic scientific methods by which the research into the subject proceeded. And every book examines the practical applications of an invention, branch of science, or scientific principle in industry, public health, and personal life, as well as potential future uses and effects based on ongoing research. Fully documented quotations, annotated bibliographies that include both print and electronic sources, glossaries, indexes, and technical illustrations are among the supplemental features designed to point researchers to further exploration of the subject.

Facing the Ultimate Unknowable

The concept of black holes consistently grips the human imagination. Many strange and frightening creatures and objects have been invented in mythology and fiction, and modern scientists have revealed a number of equally bizarre and disquieting things in the natural world. But none of these quite compares to the idea of the black hole—an object whose gravitational pull is so great that even light cannot escape it, and a place where most of the normal laws of nature break down. In the words of noted physicist Kip Thorne, one of the world's leading experts on black holes:

> Of all the conceptions of the human mind, from unicorns to gargoyles to the hydrogen bomb, the most fantastic, perhaps, is the black hole: a hole in space with a definite edge into which anything can fall and out of which nothing can escape, a hole with a gravitational force so strong that even light is caught and held in its grip, a hole that curves space and warps time.

To many people, the very idea of such a cosmic monster on the loose seems like something out of a science fiction novel or movie. And yet, says Thorne, "well-tested laws of physics predict firmly that black holes exist. In our galaxy alone there may be millions."[1]

Mysterious Monsters

In spite of the possibly large number of black holes lurking out there, however, these strange objects are far from easy to observe and study. Thorne admits, "Their darkness hides them from view. Astronomers have great difficulty finding them."[2] This elusiveness imparts to black holes an air of mystery. And indeed, one reason they are so fascinating to so many people is that they are exceedingly mysterious objects. Because even light is trapped inside them, cutting them off from the visible and tangible parts of the universe, they are dark, foreboding, and in some

Gas and rocky debris swirl around a black hole, creating a disk of material that will eventually be drawn inside the hole.

ways frightening. Most importantly, what lies inside black holes, no matter how hard humans try to theorize about it, is ultimately unknowable. As eminent scholar John Taylor, of King's College, London, puts it:

> Ever since humans began to think, we have worshiped that which we cannot understand. As millennia have passed, we have understood an ever-increasing amount about the world around us. . . . Yet we are now in a position of facing the ultimate unknowable, which can never be penetrated as long as we remain in our present physical form. The ultimate unknowable is the black hole. However hard we may struggle, we will never be able to get out of this most fearsome object of the heavens once inside it. Nor can we ever find out what is happening in its interior if we stay outside, fearing to make the one-way trip.[3]

Why Study Black Holes?

If black holes are so mysterious and in many ways unknowable, it is only natural for the layperson to wonder if they are worth studying at all. Would it not make more sense for astronomers to spend their time, energy, and money pursuing more practical endeavors? The answer to this question is a resounding no. More and more evidence suggests that black holes are intimately connected to many of the most fundamental processes of the universe. First, these objects are manifestations of ordinary gravity working overtime, so to speak. Gravity is the force that holds the universe together, and the more that scientists can learn about gravity, the better they can explain the origins and structure of the universe. "A strong motivation for searching for black holes," physicists Mitchell Begelman and Martin Rees write, "is that they represent objects where gravity has overwhelmed all other forces, allowing one to test theories of gravitation under the most extreme conditions."[4]

Among the other reasons that scientists are eager to learn more about black holes is the fact that many of these objects evolved from ordinary stars. Understanding how black holes form from stars tells much about the final stages of stellar evolution. (The term "stellar" refers to stars.) Also, increasing evidence points to the possibility that the evolution of galaxies—large swirling masses made up of billions of stars—may be inexorably tied to the formation and life cycles of gigantic black holes occupying their central regions.

In addition, scientists now believe that black holes may contain important clues to the nature of the relationship between space and time, that is, between the familiar three-dimensional world and the fourth dimension—time. Scientists often refer to the interaction of space and time as "spacetime." Near black holes, "spacetime behaves in peculiar and highly 'non-intuitive' ways," Begelman points out:

> For instance, time would "stand still" for an observer who, managing to hover or orbit just outside the horizon [the outer edge of a black hole], could then see the whole future of the external universe in what, to him, was quite a short period. Stranger things might happen if one ventured inside the horizon. . . . Our uncertainty about the "interior" of black holes doesn't reduce our confidence in predicting their astrophysical consequences [effects on the universe around them]. As an analogy, there are many mysteries deep inside the atomic nucleus, but this realization doesn't prevent physicists from calculating the properties of atoms.[5]

Thus, black holes seem to be closely connected to many of the basic properties and processes of the universe. Evidence shows, for example, that gravity,

stellar evolution, the formation of galaxies, and the effects of time on space (and vice versa) are all associated in various ways with these cosmic monsters. And the search for answers to the many riddles of black holes is opening up an exciting new chapter in the ongoing saga of science.

Researchers put the finishing touches on an instrument that detects X-rays, a kind of radiation that can reveal a black hole's location.

Chapter 1

Gravity and Early Predictions of Black Holes

Just about everyone has heard of black holes. But many nonscientists are not exactly sure what these bizarre objects are and what they are capable of doing. This is partly because their name can be somewhat misleading. A black hole is not simply an empty hole, or void, in space, but instead a cosmic entity having very substantial mass. (Mass is the measurable quantity of matter possessed by physical objects.) A black hole does have a hole, or tunnel, as part of its structure; but unlike a void, it possesses a number of physical properties as well, some of which can be measured by human instruments.

For example, a black hole's large mass generates an equally large gravitational field, which scientists can detect. Gravity is a force or property of all matter that attracts one object to another. In small objects such as molecules, pebbles, people, houses, and so forth, gravitational attractions are very slight and neither noticeable to the human senses nor measurable by instruments; only on planetary and larger scales do these attractions become obvious and easily measurable. Thus, Earth's gravity holds the Moon in orbit around the planet, and the gravity of the

Sun, the star at the center of our solar system, keeps Earth and the other planets in orbit around it. Likewise, a black hole exerts a gravitational attraction on any objects that happen to stray too close to it. "In fact," writes astronomer Thomas T. Arny,

> the gravitational field generated by a black hole is no different from that generated by any other body of the same mass. For example, if the sun were suddenly to become a black hole with the same mass it has now [something that could not actually happen], the Earth would continue to orbit it just as it does now.[6]

"Creatures of Gravity"

Not only do black holes exert large gravitational pulls, they also form through a process in which gravity crushes an enormous amount of material into a very small amount of space. This makes a black hole an extremely dense, or compact, object. So dense and massive is such an object that its gravity is far stronger than that of ordinary planets and stars, which have much less mass. Indeed, a black

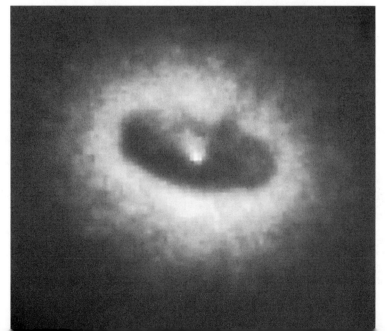

A photo of the center of a distant galaxy reveals clouds of swirling gases. Astronomers think the gas cloud in the center hides a black hole.

hole's gravity is so intense that it can even imprison light, which moves at nature's highest possible speed. This is why a black hole appears black—no light escapes it to reveal its presence to human eyes and telescopes.

Considering this close relationship between black holes and gravity, black holes might be said to be "creatures of gravity." It is not possible, therefore, to discuss black holes without understanding how gravity works, especially under extreme conditions. In fact, it was during the years immediately following the discovery of how gravity works that scientists first predicted the existence of black holes, although at the time they were not called black holes and not a shred of evidence for them yet existed.

The Discovery of Universal Gravitation

The first major theory of gravity came in 1666. Before this date, scientists assumed that the force that keeps people, houses, trees, and mountains firmly in place on Earth and the force that keeps the Earth in orbit around the Sun were separate and distinct attractions. Then a brilliant young Englishman named Isaac Newton showed that this was not the case; at the same time, he demonstrated how gravity actually works.

English scientist Isaac Newton introduced a mathematical formula to measure the gravitational pull of objects.

According to Newton, he got his first major clue to gravity's identity when he witnessed an apple falling from a tree. He was not surprised that the apple fell and struck the ground, of course, since it had long been common knowledge that some mysterious power drew all objects toward the center of the Earth. What suddenly piqued Newton's interest was the concept of distance as it related to the mystery force. It occurred to him that if he stood at the top of the tallest mountain in the world and tossed out an apple, the apple would fall to the ground just as surely as it did from the branch of the tree. This meant that the mystery force was strong enough to pull on objects over distances of tens of thousands of feet. Perhaps, then, that force might pull on objects lying much farther away.

This naturally led Newton to think about the Moon, which was clearly hundreds of thousands of miles away from Earth. Maybe, he reasoned, the same force that caused the apple to fall was pulling on the Moon. In that case, the Moon was "falling" toward Earth and the only reason the two objects did not collide was that the Moon's rapid motion outward, into space, cancelled out, or balanced, the attraction of the mystery force. From this logical (and as it turned out, correct) realization, it was not a great leap to suppose that the very same force kept Earth and the other planets in orbit around the Sun. Newton concluded that the mystery force, which he called gravity, existed throughout the universe, and was therefore universal. And appropriately, he dubbed his new theory the law of universal gravitation.

Through an elegant mathematical formula, Newton demonstrated that the gravitational pull exerted between two objects depends on two factors—the mass of the objects and the distance separating them. A small object with very little mass, he showed, exerts very little attraction on another object; a very large and massive object, such as a planet, exerts a measurable gravitational pull on another object. At the same time, distance comes into play. The farther apart two objects are, Newton showed, the less their gravities attract each other. And the reverse is also true—the closer the two objects are, the stronger they attract each other. This explains why the Sun easily maintains its hold on Earth, which lies relatively near the star, while the Sun's gravity has no measurable effect on other stars, which exist at distances thousands of times greater than that between the Sun and Earth.

Newton's theory of universal gravitation revolutionized the physical sciences, especially the disciplines of physics and astronomy. As noted science writer John Gribbin states it:

> Newton really had explained the fall of an apple and the motion of the Moon with one set of laws. In doing so, he removed the mystery from the behavior of heavenly bodies, and opened the eyes of scientists to the fact that the behavior of the stars and planets—the behavior of the whole universe—might be explained using the same laws of physics that are derived from studies carried out in laboratories on Earth.[7]

Escape Velocity and Invisible Stars

One of the many implications of Newton's gravitational theory almost inevitably led to the basic concept of what are today called black holes. While studying gravitational attraction, some of his immediate scientific successors considered what requirements would be needed to overcome that attraction. Newton's formula showed why Earth remains in orbit around the Sun and does not fall onto the star; namely, the planet moves away from the Sun at just the right speed to match and balance its great gravitational pull. But what if Earth could suddenly move faster, some scientists wondered? Logically, it would then be able to overcome the Sun's gravity and escape from the star's grip.

The speed at which an object must move in order to escape the gravity of another object became known as its escape velocity. Earth's escape velocity, for instance, is about seven miles per second, which means that a rocket or space shuttle must achieve that speed to escape the pull of Earth's gravity. In contrast, a rocket blasting off from Jupiter at seven miles per second would not be able to escape that planet. This is because Jupiter is a good deal more massive than Earth and therefore has much stronger gravity. "The escape velocity is different for different worlds," renowned science writer Isaac Asimov explains.

> A world that is less massive than Earth . . . has a lower escape velocity from its surface. . . . On the other hand, worlds that are more massive than Earth have higher escape velocities than it has. It is not surprising that the giant of the planetary system, Jupiter, has the highest escape velocity. . . . From Jupiter's surface, the escape velocity is . . . 5.4 times that from Earth's surface.[8]

During the 1700s, a few scientists gave considerable thought to this idea of more massive objects

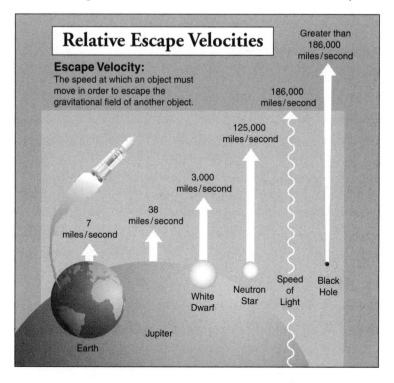

Relative Escape Velocities

Greater than 186,000 miles/second

Escape Velocity:
The speed at which an object must move in order to escape the gravitational field of another object.

186,000 miles/second

125,000 miles/second

3,000 miles/second

38 miles/second

7 miles/second

White Dwarf

Neutron Star

Speed of Light

Black Hole

Jupiter

Earth

John Michell:
the Forgotten Pioneer

The first person to realize that objects like black holes might exist—
English scientist John Michell—is all but forgotten now, except by
astronomers. In this excerpt from *In Search of the Edge of Time*,
noted science writer John Gribbin summarizes Michell's career and
contributions to science.

Born in 1724, Michell . . . is still known as the father of the science of seismology [the study of earthquakes]. He studied at the
University of Cambridge, graduating in 1752, and his interest in
earthquakes was stimulated by the disastrous seismic shock that
struck Lisbon [Portugal] in 1755. Michell established that the
damage had actually been caused by an earthquake centered
underneath the Atlantic Ocean. He became Woodwardian
Professor of Geology at Cambridge in 1762, a year after becom-
ing a bachelor of divinity. . . . Michell made many contributions
to astronomy, including the first realistic estimate of the distance to the stars, and the suggestion that some pairs of stars
seen in the night sky . . . are really "binary stars," in orbit around
each other. . . . The first mention of dark stars [i.e., black holes]
was made in a paper by Michell read to the Royal Society . . . in
1783. This was an impressively detailed discussion of ways to
work out the properties of stars, including their distances, sizes,
and masses, by measuring the gravitational effect of light emitted from their surfaces.

having higher escape velocities. One of these researchers was English astronomer John Michell, who
carried out a detailed study of the properties of stars.
It was by then clear that some stars in the heavens
are more massive than the Sun. Michell did not
know if there is an upper limit to a star's size. But at
least in theory, he proposed, stars with truly tremendous mass might exist, and if so, their gravities
would be huge. Moreover, the escape velocities of
such giant stars would be correspondingly huge.

That led Michell to ponder just how high a star's
escape velocity could reach. And taking this line of
reasoning to its logical extreme, he wondered what
might happen if the star's escape velocity exceeded
the speed of light—186,000 miles per second. In that

case, he reasoned, even light could not escape the star. In a paper published in 1784, he wrote: "If there should really exist in nature any bodies whose . . . diameters are more than 500 times the diameter of the sun," they would have enormous gravities and escape velocities. Thus, "all light emitted from such a body would be made to return to it by its own power of gravity." And because the light cannot leave the star, "we could have no information from sight."[9] In other words, the star would be dark and therefore invisible to human eyes and telescopes. Appropriately, Michell called these objects "dark stars."

Michell was not the only scientist of his day fascinated by the effects of extreme gravity. In 1795 French scientist Pierre-Simon Laplace arrived at the same basic conclusion independently. Someplace in the heavens, he wrote, there might exist

> invisible bodies as large, and perhaps in as great number, as the stars. A luminous star of the same density [compactness] as the Earth, and whose diameter was two hundred and fifty times greater than that of the sun, would not, because of its [gravitational] attraction, allow any of its [light] rays to arrive at us; it is therefore possible that the largest luminous bodies of the universe may, through this cause, be invisible.[10]

Based on this conclusion, Laplace called these hypothetical objects *les corps obscures*, or "invisible bodies."

Bendable Space and Gravity Wells

Michell's and Laplace's descriptions of dark stars and invisible bodies were at the time completely theoretical. They had absolutely no evidence for these strange celestial bodies, and the vast majority of scientists thought that no such bodies existed. Not surprisingly, therefore, these precursors of black holes became a mere mathematical curiosity. And for more than a century afterward few scientists gave them any thought.

In the early twentieth century, however, the concept of black holes enjoyed an unexpected revival when a brilliant young German scientist named Albert Einstein proposed a new theory of gravity. Part of his general theory of relativity, published in 1915–1916, it did not disprove Newton's theory and formula for universal gravitation. Rather, Einstein's version simply explained the nature of space and the way gravity works within it differently than Newton's had.

For example, according to Newton gravity is a force exerted by objects and therefore emanates somehow from their centers. According to Einstein, however, gravity is not a directed force but a property of space itself, an idea that was revolutionary because it proposed that space actually has an unseen structure. Before Einstein, the common assumption among physicists and other scientists was that space is an empty void with no ability to affect the bodies moving within it. In contrast, Einstein argued that space has an invisible "fabric" with an elastic, or bendable, quality.

Further, Einstein stated, bodies possessing mass move through space and interact with its hidden fabric by sinking into it and creating a depression. Scientists came to call such a well-like depression a "gravity well." In this view, the depth of a gravity well depends on a body's mass; obviously, the more massive the body is, the deeper the body will sink and the deeper the well it will create. In this way, said Einstein, very massive objects, like planets and stars, distort or curve space's elastic fabric, and this curvature is what people experience as gravity. Arny gives this simplified analogy:

Imagine a waterbed on which you have placed a baseball. The baseball makes a small depression

Einstein:
Visionary of Space and Time

No other scientist has contributed more to human understanding of the behavior of light, the curvature of space, and the existence of black holes than physicist Albert Einstein. He was born in Ulm, Germany, in 1879. Soon his father, who manufactured electronic goods, moved the family to Munich, and later to Milan, Italy. As a young man, Albert studied in Switzerland and in 1900 graduated from Zurich Polytechnic Institute.

In 1905 he published three ground-breaking scientific papers, one on the nature of light, another on the mechanics of atom-sized molecules, and a third stating most of the principles that came to be known as his special theory of relativity. Perhaps the most famous component of the theory of special relativity is that mass and energy are equivalent. In 1915 Einstein published his visionary general theory of relativity, in which he showed that gravity is a function of four-dimensional space and time and that space is curved. Among the equations for general relativity were some that predicted the existence of black holes.

Einstein received the Nobel Prize in physics in 1921 and died in 1955. Throughout the twentieth century, one scientific experiment and discovery after another verified his predictions with amazing accuracy, including the discovery of black holes. Today he is regarded as one of the greatest scientists in history.

Physicist Albert Einstein's ideas about matter, energy, and time proved revolutionary.

in the otherwise flat surface of the bed. If a marble is now placed near the baseball, it will roll along the curved surface into the depression. The bending of its environment made by the baseball therefore creates an "attraction" between the baseball and the marble. Now suppose we replace the baseball with a bowling ball. It will make a bigger depression and the marble will roll in further and be moving faster as it hits the bottom. We therefore infer from the analogy that the strength of the attraction between the bodies depends on the amount by which the surface is curved. Gravity also behaves this way, according to the general theory of relativity. According to that theory, mass creates a curvature of space, and gravitational motion occurs as bodies move along the curvature.[11]

Now replace this analogy with one involving real objects moving through outer space. Consider two planets of differing size approaching each other. The smaller planet encounters the curve of the larger planet's gravity well and rolls "downhill" toward the

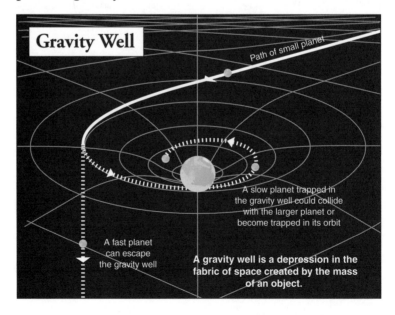

Gravity Well

Path of small planet

A slow planet trapped in the gravity well could collide with the larger planet or become trapped in its orbit

A fast planet can escape the gravity well

A gravity well is a depression in the fabric of space created by the mass of an object.

larger object. (This produces exactly the same effect as the larger planet "pulling in" the smaller one in Newton's gravitational model, so Newton's formula can still be applied and its results for most objects are still valid.) In Einstein's gravitational model, if the smaller planet is moving fast enough, it will soon roll out of the larger planet's gravity well and continue on its way. If it is not moving at the proper escape velocity, however, it will be trapped in the well, in which case it will either go into orbit around the larger planet or crash into it.

Could Superdense Bodies Exist?

The new theory of curved space created a great stir in scientific circles. Many physicists, astronomers, and other scientists felt that Einstein's ideas were compelling and they wanted to test and prove the theory. If space is indeed curved and massive bodies create gravity wells, they reasoned, a very deep gravity well should deflect a beam of light. In other words, though light travels swiftly enough to allow it to escape such a well, the well should bend the beam enough for scientists to measure it.

What was needed for the test was a very massive body, at least by human standards. And because it is the largest object in the solar system, the Sun was the logical choice. The historic experiment took place on May 29, 1919, during a solar eclipse that was visible from the western coast of central Africa. "Bright stars were visible in the sky near the eclipsed sun," Asimov explains, "and their light on its way to Earth skimmed past the sun. Einstein's theory predicted that this light would be bent very slightly toward the sun as it passed."[12] Sure enough, after analyzing the data gathered during the eclipse, astronomers found that the light from the more distant stars did bend slightly as it passed by the Sun. In fact, the light beams were deflected by nearly the exact amount Einstein had predicted.

Einstein's theory of curved space had been confirmed. (Several other experiments proving the validity of his general theory of relativity have been conducted since that time.) The theory of relativity also forced scientists to readdress the questions raised long before by Michell and Laplace about the extreme effects of gravity. The experiment during the eclipse had demonstrated that the Sun's gravity well bends light slightly. It stood to reason, therefore, that a much more massive object would bend light even more. And this naturally led to the theoretical possibility that supermassive, superdense bodies might exist. If so, such a body would possess an extremely deep gravity well, perhaps so deep that light could not escape. In 1939 physicist J. Robert Oppenheimer and his student George M. Volkoff published a scientific paper predicting the existence of superdense stars that would have extremely deep, perhaps even bottomless, gravity wells.

Yet there was still no direct observational proof of such bizarre cosmic bodies. So in the years that followed, the concept of dark stars and their poten-

This photo taken by the Hubble Space Telescope shows a cluster of distant galaxies whose combined gravity distorts and bends the light these objects give off.

tially weird effects on space and light remained in the province of science fiction stories and films. The first attempt to deal with the idea on film was an episode of the original *Star Trek* television series first broadcast in 1967. *Star Trek*'s Captain Kirk and his crew referred to the strange object they encountered as a "black star," which turned out to be prophetic. At the time, interest in such objects was reviving among a handful of physicists, and only a few months after the *Star Trek* episode aired, noted Princeton University physicist John A. Wheeler coined the term "black hole." The name was perfectly descriptive and highly catchy, and it immediately became popular. Thereafter, the concept of black holes captured the attention of increasing numbers of physicists, astronomers, and other scientists, as well as science fiction fans. As Wheeler himself later remarked:

> The advent of the term black hole in 1967 was terminologically trivial but psychologically powerful. After the name was introduced, more and more astronomers and astrophysicists came to appreciate that black holes might not be a figment of the imagination but astronomical objects worth spending time and money to seek.[13]

Indeed, time and money turned out to be important keys to unlocking the secrets of black holes. Their prediction in theory by scientists over the course of nearly two centuries had been only a first step. The next necessary steps, or goals, were: more serious and concentrated study of the concept, including a better understanding of how these strange objects form; and a serious attempt to detect them. Since the late 1960s, these goals have been largely fulfilled by a series of exciting researches and discoveries that have significantly altered and improved human understanding of the universe.

Chapter 2

Dying Stars and the Formation of Black Holes

Twentieth-century predictions that black holes might exist naturally raised the question of how such superdense objects could form. Over time, scientists came to realize that there might be more than one answer to this question, depending on the size of the black hole. Ever since the days of Michell and Laplace, astronomers and physicists had focused their attention on star-sized objects with extreme gravity. So the quest to understand how such bodies form concentrated on the life cycles of and physical processes within stars.

However, the mathematical equations of Einstein's general theory of relativity allow for the existence of black holes of any size, including very small ones. After John Wheeler coined the term black hole in 1967, a number of scientists began theorizing about miniature black holes. A mini–black hole might be the size of an atom. Yet its matter would be so densely compacted that it would weigh something like 100 trillion tons! An even tinier black hole—say the size of an atom's nucleus—would still tip the scales at about a billion tons.

Miniature and Stellar Black Holes

Such mini–black holes would have no obvious con-nection with star-sized, or stellar, black holes. So the formation of the smaller version likely has nothing to do with the life and death of stars. What force or process, then, could have created mini–black holes? In the early 1970s, noted British physicist Stephen Hawking offered a believable answer, namely that these tiny superdense objects came into being dur-ing the Big Bang—the enormous explosion in which, most scientists believe, the known universe was created. "With vast quantities of matter explod-ing all over the place," Isaac Asimov explains,

Stephen Hawking proposed that microscopic black holes formed in the huge explosion that gave birth to the universe.

some different sections of the expanding substance [i.e., matter] might collide. Part of this colliding matter might then be squeezed together under enormous pressure from all sides. The squeezed matter might shrink to a point where the mounting gravitational intensity would keep it shrunk forever.[14]

Hawking and others think that millions of such mini–black holes might still exist in various parts of the universe. If so, sooner or later a few might come close to an asteroid, planet, or other large solid body and be drawn to it by its gravity. Such a cosmic meeting would probably be neither dangerous nor catastrophic, however. According to Asimov:

If a mini–black hole collides with a larger body, it will simply bore its way through. It will engulf the first bit of matter with which it collides, liberating enough energy in the process to melt and vaporize the matter immediately ahead. It will then pass through the hot vapor, absorbing it as it goes and adding to the heat, emerging at last as a considerably larger black hole than it was when it entered.[15]

The channel cut through a planet by a mini–black hole would be so small and narrow that it would be far less noticeable or consequential than a tunnel dug through a garden by an ant. If mini–black holes do exist, therefore, their physical effects on large bodies are minimal and they are of little concern to human beings and any other living beings inhabiting the universe.

By contrast, black holes of stellar and larger masses have far more important potential consequences for the universe and life. And this is why scientists have devoted so much time and effort in recent years to understanding how they form, as well as their properties. They realized that it would require a tremendously violent process or event to compress such gigantic quantities of matter into an extremely small space. Moreover, the energy produced would have to be millions of times larger than in those events people normally deem catastrophic—including earthquakes, volcanic eruptions, and the crash of asteroids onto planetary surfaces. It became clear to scientists that only the phenomenally violent death of a large star could account for the creation of a stellar black hole.

The Life Cycles of Stars

Understanding how stars die and create superdense bodies requires some basic knowledge of how stars live. In the same way that people undergo an inevitable life cycle, stars are born, live out their lives, and finally die. The nursery of a typical star, including one like the Sun, is an extremely large cloud of gases and dust floating through space. Such clouds come into being when "winds" created by exploding stars blow scattered molecules of gas and particles of dust around; some become even more scattered, while others become more concentrated. When such a cloud becomes concentrated enough, gravity causes it to contract still further over time. This contraction also produces heat, which makes the gases and dust grow steadily hotter. Soon, the center of the cloud becomes hot enough to cook a steak; then it reaches the temperature of a blast furnace; and finally, after a few million years, the temperature at the cloud's core becomes hot enough to fuse hydrogen atoms and thereby ignite nuclear reactions. At that instant, the core emits a huge burst of blinding light and other energy that blows away the cooler outer layers of the cloud, leaving behind a giant ball of white-hot gases—a newborn star.

The new star has enough hydrogen in its interior to keep its self-sustaining nuclear reactions going for billions of years. And throughout this longest portion

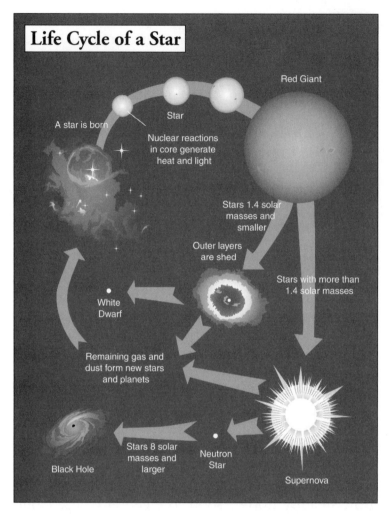

Life Cycle of a Star

Red Giant

A star is born

Star

Nuclear reactions in core generate heat and light

Stars 1.4 solar masses and smaller

Outer layers are shed

White Dwarf

Stars with more than 1.4 solar masses

Remaining gas and dust form new stars and planets

Black Hole

Stars 8 solar masses and larger

Neutron Star

Supernova

of its life cycle, it continues producing light and heat. If certain other factors in the star's solar system are favorable—such as the formation of a planet at the right distance from the star and the presence of water—this abundant light and heat makes the rise of life possible in that solar system. No significant danger is posed to such life as long as the star remains stable.

The reason a typical star can remain stable for so long is that two enormous forces occurring within the body of the object oppose each other, creating an equilibrium, or balance. One of these forces is gravity, which makes the massive quantities of matter in the star's outer layers fall inward, creating great pressure. The Sun "contains a thousand times more mass than Jupiter," Begelman and Rees point out. If the Sun were a cold body, "gravity would compress it to a million times the density of an ordinary solid. It would be . . . about the same size as the Earth, but 330,000 times more massive."[16]

But as everyone can easily see and feel, the Sun is not a cold body. Stars like the Sun produce enormous amounts of energy, accounting for the second major force at work within them. The nuclear reactions taking place in a star's core release immense amounts of heat, light, and tiny particles that travel outward toward the surface. In the Sun, for example, each and every second the core produces the same amount of energy as 100 million nuclear bombs exploding simultaneously. As this terrific stream of energy moves outward from the core, it exerts a huge amount of outward pressure. And that pressure balances the force of gravity pushing inward. The Sun's center, Begelman and Rees summarize,

> has a temperature of about 15 million degrees . . . thousands of times hotter even than its glowing surface. At these high temperatures, the atomic nuclei inside the sun are moving randomly at speeds of hundreds of kilometers per second. It is the pressure of this hot interior . . . that counteracts the [internal] effect of gravity in all stars like the sun.[17]

Thanks to this balance between outward and inward pressures, stars like the Sun maintain their structures and remain stable for long periods of time. Astronomers estimate that the Sun, which has been in this stable state for several billion years, will remain in it for several billion years to come. Like an animal or a person, however, the great luminous ball cannot live forever. Eventually, a star must use up all of its fuel and enter its death throes, producing a catastrophe in which most of its matter is forced into an extremely dense state. This state can take one of three different forms, depending on the star's initial mass; in each case, a superdense object is created. Two of these objects—a white dwarf and a neutron star—are in a sense immediate precursors of and steps on the road to the black hole. The third is the black hole itself.

Step One: White Dwarfs

The Sun is destined to be transformed into the first of the three superdense bodies created when a star dies, a white dwarf. Billions of years from now, our star will begin to run out of the hydrogen that fuels the nuclear reactions in its core. When most of the hydrogen is gone, the core will get both denser and hotter. This extra heat will cause the Sun's outer layers to expand outward, transforming it into an enormous star hundreds of times bigger than it is now; in fact, its surface will engulf the orbits of Mercury and Venus, destroying those planets, and the surface of Earth (which will then be the innermost planet in the solar system) will be scorched as if in a blast furnace. However, because the Sun's new surface will be stretched and more spread out than before, any given portion of it will be a bit cooler. So the star's color will change from a hot yellow to a cooler red. For this reason such expanded, cooler stars are called red giants.

Eventually, the core of the red giant Sun will completely run out of hydrogen, at which point it will start burning the next heaviest element, helium. Of course, the helium will soon get used up, too, and in time the star will no longer burn fuel to produce nuclear reactions. At that point, the delicate balance that keeps the star stable will be undermined. The outward pressure of escaping energy will decrease, allowing it to be overcome by the inward pressure of

Explosions on White Dwarfs

Once formed by stellar collapse, solitary white dwarfs slowly cool and fade from view. If they are part of binary (double-star) systems, however, white dwarfs can periodically produce explosions called novas, as explained here by University of Amherst astronomer Thomas T. Arny in his noted astronomy text *Explorations*.

If a white dwarf has a nearby companion, gas expelled from the companion may fall onto the dwarf. . . . Coming from the companion's outer layers, such gas is rich in hydrogen and may briefly replenish the white dwarf's fuel supply. The new fuel forms a layer on the white dwarf's surface, where gravity compresses and heats it. The gas layer eventually reaches the ignition temperature for hydrogen, but . . . nuclear burning in a degenerate gas can be explosive. The detonating hydrogen is blasted into space and forms an expanding shell of hot gas . . . that radiates far more energy than the white dwarf itself. Sometimes these stellar explosions are visible to the naked eye. When earlier astronomers saw such events, they called them novas, from the Latin word for "new," because the explosion would make a bright point of light appear in the sky where no star was previously visible.

The white dwarf's strong gravitational pull draws gas and other matter from the nearby star.

Gas and matter accumulate and are heated on the white dwarf's surface.

The heated matter ignites and explodes, causing a bright, shell-like blast called a nova.

gravity. "Gravitation has been waiting," Asimov writes, "pulling patiently and tirelessly for many billions of years, and finally resistance to that pull has collapsed."[18]

As gravity takes over, the red giant Sun will start to shrink. Some of its outer material will escape into space. But most will remain inside the shrinking star, which, compelled by gravity's mighty hand, will finally crush this matter into a white dwarf—a small, hot, but only dimly luminous ball about the size of Earth. A white dwarf is so dense that a mere tablespoon of its material weighs a thousand tons. Thus it comes as no surprise that such a body possesses a very deep gravity well and therefore a powerful gravitational pull. To escape a white dwarf, a spaceship would need to reach a speed of about three thousand miles per second! (Of course, it would be foolhardy to land on a white dwarf in the first place, since its gravity would quickly crush the ship and its occupants into flattened deposits of debris.)

Step Two: Neutron Stars

Astronomers have determined that the ultimate fate of average-sized stars—those having up to 1.4 times the mass of the Sun (or 1.4 solar masses)—is to become white dwarfs. But what about stars that start out with more than 1.4 solar masses? They obviously have stronger gravities. So it is only logical that their end will be more violent and result in the formation of an object even more dense than a white dwarf.

Indeed, a star possessing between 1.4 and perhaps 8 solar masses bypasses the white dwarf stage and proceeds to the next stop on the road to the black hole. (Scientists still differ on the mass of stars that will become neutron stars. Other estimates include 1.4 to 3.2 and 1.4 to 5 solar masses.) This heavier star goes through the same initial steps as a Sun-sized star—depletion of hydrogen, expansion into a red giant, and the burning of helium. But after that, things happen very differently, as Begelman and Rees explain:

> Massive stars are powered in later life by a sequence of nuclear reactions involving heavier and heavier elements. As each nuclear fuel is exhausted—hydrogen fused into helium, then helium into carbon and oxygen, etc.—the inner part of the star contracts becoming even hotter. . . . This process would proceed all the way up to iron. At every stage up to this point, the creation of heavier atomic nuclei releases energy that staves off gravitational collapse. But there are no nuclear reactions that can release energy from iron; iron is the end of the nuclear road for a star. What happens next is one of the most spectacular events known in astronomy. . . . Since there are no nuclear reactions that can extract energy from iron, the supply of fuel is shut off and the core suffers sudden and catastrophic collapse . . . in a fraction of a second. . . . The density of the collapsing core becomes so great that the protons and electrons [the charged particles of its atoms] are fused together to form neutrons, electrically neutral subatomic particles.[19]

Because such an object is made up almost entirely of neutrons (forming a substance many scientists call neutronium), it is called a neutron star.

The collapse that creates a neutron star is so violent that it triggers a secondary catastrophe—a stupendous explosion. In this spectacular outburst, called a supernova, significant portions of the star's outer layers blast away into space. This material forms a gaseous shell, often referred to as a supernova remnant, that expands outward for thousands or even millions of years, growing increasingly thinner. (It grows fainter, too, except when lit up by the glow of any stars it passes.)

The bright object at the center of the Crab Nebula is the pulsar discovered in 1968. Such objects are actually neutron stars.

The rest of the star's original mass is now concentrated in a ball of neutronium about ten to twenty miles across, roughly the size of a large city. So dense is the material in a neutron star that a tablespoon of it weighs at least several trillion tons. Furthermore, such a star's escape velocity is nearly 125,000 miles per second, about two-thirds the speed of light.

All of this sounds convincing in theory. But astronomers had no direct proof of the existence of neutron stars until the late 1960s, when objects called pulsars began to be found. In 1968, for example, astronomers discovered a strange object at the center of the Crab Nebula. Located in the constellation of Taurus, the bull, this bright, rapidly expanding cloud of gases is the remnant of a supernova that occurred in 1054 and was recorded by Chinese and

Japanese observers. Modern astronomers noted that the object at the center of the nebula gives off regular, intense bursts, or pulses, of radiation at the rate of thirty per second. Appropriately, they named this and other similar objects pulsars.

It soon became clear that pulsars are neutron stars, which rotate (spin) at incredible speeds. This rapid rotation is caused by the enormous inward rush of energy that occurs during the star's collapse into a superdense ball. As for why a neutron star pulsates energy, noted astronomer Herbert Friedman writes:

> When a neutron star collapses, it also drags with it the original stellar magnetic field until it is concentrated one billion-fold at the surface of the neutron star. In the tight grip of such a strong field, plasma [hot gases] at the magnetic poles would be whipped around with the spinning star. This whirling plasma could generate

Instant Death on a Neutron Star

Neutron stars have enormous gravity, which would cause a living creature to be crushed out of existence in a fraction of a second, as explained by the great science explainer Isaac Asimov in his book *The Collapsing Universe*.

> Suppose that an object with the mass of the sun collapses to the neutron-star stage and is only 14 kilometers [8.7 miles] in diameter. An object on its surface will now be only 1/100,000 the distance to its center as it would be if it were on the surface of the sun. The tidal effect on the neutron star's surface is therefore 100,000 X 100,000 X 100,000 times that on the sun's surface, or a million billion times that on the sun's surface and a quarter of a million billion times that on the Earth's surface. A two-meter-tall human being standing on a neutron star and immune to its radiation, heat, or total gravity would nevertheless be stretched apart by a force of 18 billion kilograms in the direction toward and away from the neutron star's center, and of course the human being, or anything else, would fly apart into dust-sized particles.

[a] highly directional radio emission [i.e., radiation shooting out of a specific location on the star] that would beam into space like the light of a rotating searchlight beacon atop a lighthouse. As the radio beam sweeps over the Earth, our radio telescopes record repeated flashes.[20]

Step Three: Stellar Black Holes

Scientists now know that neutron stars like the one in the Crab Nebula are not the last word, so to speak, in the awesome story of stellar collapse. That distinction belongs to the black hole. Light is just barely able to escape the deep gravity well of a neutron star, so in a sense it almost qualifies for black hole status. In fact, says John Gribbin, "A neutron star sits on the very threshold of being a black hole."[21] One major factor that sets black holes apart from neutron stars, however, is that *no* light can escape from a black hole; light and everything else that gets too close to a black hole becomes trapped inside its gravity well forever.

A stellar black hole forms from the collapse of a star having more than eight times the mass of the Sun. So powerful is the force of the inrushing matter that it bypasses both the white dwarf and neutron star stages and compresses that matter into an even denser state. In fact, the matter keeps on falling down the star's gravity well in a sort of neverending death spiral. This is because the gravity well of a black hole is like a bottomless pit, from which nothing can escape.

Not surprisingly, this densest of superdense objects jams an extremely large amount of material into a very small volume of space. A stellar black hole is surprisingly small, therefore. One formed during the death of a star having eight solar masses would probably be only about the size of a small house. It is important to remember that most of the former star's original matter is still inside the black hole. (Some of its matter was ejected into space during the supernova accompanying the star's collapse.) That means that the object's gravitational pull will be roughly the same as that of the original star. Any planets orbiting the star before its collapse would continue orbiting the black hole, which would not capture and consume them unless they strayed too close to it.

The survival of a planet and the survival of living things that might inhabit it are two different things, however. A majority of life forms that happen to exist on planets orbiting a star that becomes a black hole will die from powerful radiation released during the catastrophic collapse and supernova. And any life that has the misfortune to survive this disaster will quickly freeze to death after the star stops radiating light and heat. Clearly, the formation of a stellar black hole is one of the most awesome and potentially lethal events that can occur in nature.

Chapter 3

Properties and Potential Uses of Black Holes

Like ordinary stars, planets, and other celestial bodies, black holes, which astronomers have been able to detect in recent years, have certain physical properties that distinguish them from the others. Yet because of a black hole's extraordinary nature, especially the fact that it is black and invisible, very few of its properties can be directly measured from the outside. "From the outside," John Gribbin explains,

> you can [calculate] the mass of the hole from its gravitational attraction and the speed with which it rotates. If it has an electric charge, you could measure that as well. But those . . . properties are *all* you can ever measure. There is no way to tell what the matter that went into the hole was before it was swallowed up . . . whether it was a star, a great glob of water, or a pile of frozen TV dinners. There is no way to distinguish a black hole made of stellar material from one made of anything else, a property summed up by [scientists] in the expression "black holes have no hair [distinct, visible physical characteristics]," coined by [John] Wheeler and his colleague Kip Thorne in the early 1970s.[22]

Still, even if black holes "have no hair," they do behave in certain definite and characteristic ways as they interact with the universe around them. By observing this behavior, scientists can theorize and draw conclusions about those properties of black holes that cannot be seen or measured directly. And the more people learn about these cosmic oddities, the more they will be able to reveal the hidden secrets of the universe. Moreover, learning as much as possible about the properties of black holes could conceivably prove beneficial to humanity. Someday it may be possible to harness and utilize some of the vast energies produced by these objects.

Calculating a Black Hole's Mass and Radius

The first and probably most obvious measurable property of a black hole is its mass. Clearly, black holes must be extremely massive and also dense, since each consists of most of the matter of a giant star compressed into an unimaginably tiny space.

Kip Thorne of the California Institute of Technology is one of the leading experts on black holes and their strange properties.

Yet how can scientists on Earth measure the mass of a black hole or other body lying trillions of miles away? That depends on whether any stars or other large bodies happen to lie near the black hole. If it is floating through space alone, far from any such objects, scientists will have no way to measure its mass.

In contrast, if the black hole and a star are orbiting each other (actually, each orbiting a common center of gravity), scientists can use the formula for universal gravitation to compute their masses. First, using sensitive instruments and mathematics, they measure the distance between the two objects. Then they compute their orbital velocity (the speed at which they move in orbit). Finally, they plug these figures into an equation that determines the mass. As Thomas Arny says, this method "can be used to find the mass of any body around which another object orbits. Thus, gravity becomes a tool for determining the mass of astronomical bodies."[23] In the case of black holes, scientists often express their masses in multiples of the Sun's mass. A black hole is said to contain 8, 12, 20, or some other number of solar masses.

The mass of a black hole, which is measurable, directly affects the nature of other properties of the hole that are *not* measurable. One of these is the size of its Schwarzschild radius. The easiest way to understand this fundamental property of a black hole is to visualize the hole moving through space. From time to time, it encounters gas, dust, asteroids, and other forms of matter, which are naturally attracted by its huge gravitational pull. When the matter gets close enough, it is torn apart and reduced to atoms; then it is sucked into the black hole, where the debris spirals into the bottomless gravity well, never to be seen again.

The crucial part of this scenario of annihilation is that, on its way into the black hole, the matter passes what might be called "the point of no return," which scientists call the event horizon. As

Tragedy Cuts Short a Brilliant Career

German astronomer Karl Schwarzschild, who was born in 1873, made major contributions to knowledge about superdense objects and their effects on space and time. He became director of the Astrophysical Observatory in Potsdam in 1909. In 1915, while serving his country in World War I, he heard about Einstein's work on the theory of general relativity. Schwarzschild contacted Einstein and kept him informed about his own efforts to describe the geometry of spacetime around a superdense object occupying a single point, or singularity. Among Schwarzschild's mathematical discoveries was that the singularity would be separated from the event horizon by a certain distance, which scientists later named the Schwarzschild radius in his honor. Tragically, he contracted a skin disease while in the military and grew gravely ill. Einstein presented his colleague's groundbreaking ideas to the scientific community only months before Schwarzschild died in May 1916 at the age of forty-two.

long as the matter manages to stay outside the horizon, it has a chance of escaping. Once it crosses the horizon, however, it will disappear into the black hole's gravity well. The distance from the center of a black hole, called the singularity, to the event horizon is the Schwarzschild radius, named after German astronomer Karl Schwarzschild, who discovered it in 1915.

Mathematical equations show conclusively that this radius will vary according to a black hole's mass. The more massive the hole, the longer the Schwarzschild radius, and conversely, the less massive the hole, the shorter the radius. A black hole of one solar mass will have a Schwarzschild radius of 1.86 miles; and a hole of ten solar masses will have a radius of about 20 miles. In the latter case, therefore, the point of no return for any matter approaching the black hole lies 20 miles from the singularity, or center.

Putting a Spin on Black Holes

Karl Schwarzschild worked out his equations for a hypothetical black hole that does not rotate on its axis. So scientists came to call a theoretical, nonspinning black hole a Schwarzschild black hole. This model worked well enough to calculate the distance from the singularity to the event horizon. But did it accurately describe the real state of a black hole? Most physicists felt that it did not. This is because they already knew that all of the bodies ever observed in outer space both rotate and possess a measurable property known as angular momentum.

Angular momentum is the tendency of a spinning object to keep on spinning. Even if the object gets

Anatomy of a Black Hole

X-ray Gas Jets
Narrow, perpendicular jets which originate from the accretion disk. Magnetic forces or rapidly spinning gases may form pressure which shoots these jets in opposite directions.

Event Horizon
The "point of no return" where gravity becomes so strong that nothing, not even light, can escape.

Accretion Disk
Hot gas and dust orbiting around black hole forms a flattened spiral disk.

Schwarzschild Radius
Distance from the singularity to the event horizon.

Singularity
A ringlike rotating area of space which defines the black hole and is at its very center.

larger or smaller, its original rotational energy will be preserved by altering the speed of rotation appropriately. For example, when a spinning ice skater extends his or her arms, in effect making the skater's body larger, the rate of spin slows down; by contrast, when the skater draws his or her arms in tight to the body, the rate of spin increases.

This same effect can be seen when a large star collapses into a neutron star. The original star rotates at a certain rate, perhaps once every twenty or thirty days. After the collapse, its angular momentum is transferred into the much smaller neutron star, which now spins around many times in a second. It stands to reason that a black hole will follow this same scenario. Isaac Asimov summarizes it this way:

> When a star collapses, to make up for that, its speed of rotation must increase. The more extreme the collapse, the greater the gain in speed of rotation. A brand-new neutron star can spin as much as a thousand times a second. Black holes must spin more rapidly still. There's no way of avoiding that. We can say, then, that every black hole has mass and angular momentum.[24]

Thus, what was needed after Schwarzschild introduced his calculations for nonspinning black holes was a mathematical solution that would describe the workings of black holes that rotate, as all black holes are believed to do. This goal was attained in 1963 by New Zealander astronomer Roy P. Kerr, who was then working at the University of Texas. Since that time, in Kerr's honor, it has become common for scientists to refer to spinning black holes as Kerr black holes. The first definite confirmation of these objects came in August 2001, when scientists at NASA's Goddard Space Flight Center (in Greenbelt, Maryland) detected the spin of a black hole lying about ten thousand light-years from Earth. (A light-year is the distance that light travels in a year, or about 6 trillion miles.)

Accretion Disks and Shooting Gas Jets

The Kerr solution recognizes the singularity, the event horizon, the Schwarzschild radius, and other black hole properties found in the Schwarzschild solution. However, the rapid spin inherent in a Kerr black hole creates a considerably more complex and dynamic situation.

First, the singularity is not a single point, but a warped area of space shaped like a ring. Second, the event horizon, marking the boundary between the black hole and ordinary space beyond it, is moving in the same direction that the singularity is spinning. And as it moves, it drags part of the nearby region of space along with it. As Kip Thorne explains:

> The hole's spin grabs hold of its surrounding space [shaped like the bell of a trumpet] and forces it to rotate in a tornado-like manner. . . . Far from a tornado's core, the air rotates slowly, and similarly, far from the hole's [event] horizon, space rotates slowly. Near the tornado's core the air rotates fast, and similarly, near the horizon space rotates fast. At the horizon, space is locked tightly onto the horizon. It rotates at precisely the same rate as the horizon spins.[25]

At the same time, any matter that happens to lie in that area of rotating space is carried along in the moving current. The matter spins around the outside of the black hole and forms a flattened disk of material in a manner similar to that in which small pieces of rock and ice form a flattened disk of rings around the planet Saturn. Scientists call this spinning disk around a black hole an accretion disk.

The material in the accretion disk plays an important role in another effect of a black hole's spin—the creation of two narrow but powerful jets of gas that appear to be shooting out of some black holes. (In reality, the jets do not come from inside the hole; instead, they originate in the disk, outside of the event horizon.)

Astronomers have advanced a number of convincing explanations to explain how these jets might form. In one, the tremendous pressures produced by the rapidly rotating gases in the accretion disk create two vortexes, whirlpools similar to the kind formed by water swirling down a drain. These vortexes shoot jets of hot gases outward at high speeds in opposite directions.

Thorne summarizes another possible scenario for the creation of these jets. This one involves a powerful magnetic field generated by the black hole's spin:

> Magnetic field lines [invisible strands of magnetism] anchored in the [accretion] disk and

This artist's conception shows the accretion disk and gas jets of a black hole. The jets may be caused by powerful magnetic and electrical forces.

sticking out of it will be forced, by the disk's orbital motion, to spin around and around. . . . Electrical forces should anchor hot gas (plasma) onto the spinning field lines. . . . As the field lines spin, centrifugal forces [forces pushing outward] should fling the plasma outward along them to form two magnetized jets, one shooting outward and upward, the other outward and downward.[26]

The Effects of Time Dilation

Scientists have also determined that when black holes, including spinning ones, interact with normal space, they can create strange time distortions. That is, the passage of time experienced by an observer located outside a hole looking in will be markedly different from that of an observer located inside a hole looking out.

Consider the example of two astronauts in a spaceship orbiting the black hole from a safe distance. One exits the ship and propels himself toward the hole, which draws him in. From the point of view of his friend aboard the ship, he will spiral inward increasingly slowly and eventually become frozen on the hole's spinning event horizon. Round and round he will go, getting closer and closer to the horizon for years, and indeed forever; but he will never seem to pass through it into the hole. However, the point of view of the astronaut who approaches the horizon will be quite different. Time will seem to pass normally for him; he will feel himself journey from the ship to the horizon and then cross over the horizon into the black hole, all in only a few minutes.

If humanity ever develops sufficiently advanced technology, this time differential, called time dilation, might be exploited to allow people to propel themselves forward in time. (It must be emphasized that such ventures would take place outside the black hole and be unrelated to the even weirder distortions of space and time that might exist inside.) Gribbin explains how such journeys might be accomplished. A group of astronauts would bid farewell to observers on a space station orbiting far from a black hole and fly a ship toward the hole's event horizon. "The longer the astronauts spend near the event horizon, and the closer they get to it," Gribbin says,

> the stronger the effect will be. You don't even need enormously powerful rockets to take advantage of the effect, because the astronauts could use a judicious, short-lived blast on their rockets to set their spacecraft falling on an open orbit down into the region of highly distorted spacetime, leaving the observers behind. . . . The falling spacecraft would coast in . . . being accelerated by the gravity of the black hole up to the point of closest approach. Then, it would whip around the hole very sharply . . . and climb out again, now being slowed all the time by gravity. At the farthest distance from the hole, the astronauts could fire their rockets briefly again, to put the spacecraft back alongside the space station of the observers, who [would be] ready to compare clocks.[27]

When the astronauts and observers do compare clocks, they will find a noticeable difference. Whereas the astronauts may have experienced the passage of only a few hours, the observers' clocks will record that several weeks or months have gone by. If the astronauts are careful to choose just the right orbit and speed around the event horizon, they might be able to leap ahead dozens, hundreds, or even thousands of years. They could not travel backward to their starting point, however, as the effects of time dilation work in only one direction—forward (at least in ordinary space). Also, in longer journeys through time, the original observers will grow old and die

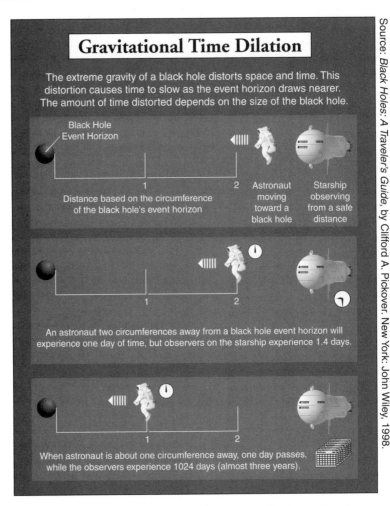

Source: *Black Holes: A Traveler's Guide*, by Clifford A. Pickover. New York: John Wiley, 1998.

Gravitational Time Dilation

The extreme gravity of a black hole distorts space and time. This distortion causes time to slow as the event horizon draws nearer. The amount of time distorted depends on the size of the black hole.

Black Hole
Event Horizon

1   2   Astronaut   Starship
Distance based on the circumference   moving   observing
of the black hole's event horizon   toward a   from a safe
                                              black hole   distance

1   2

An astronaut two circumferences away from a black hole event horizon will experience one day of time, but observers on the starship experience 1.4 days.

1   2

When astronaut is about one circumference away, one day passes, while the observers experience 1024 days (almost three years).

while the astronauts are away; so each time the travelers visit the space station, they will be greeted by a new group of observers.

Mining the Energy of Black Holes

Traveling forward in time by using the strange distortions of spacetime generated near the event horizon of a black hole may eventually become possible. Yet such undertakings would be risky and the results would be highly unpredictable and of questionable value. So a majority of people in an advanced future society may well feel that it makes more sense to exploit the unusual properties of black holes in more practical ways.

Indeed, black holes produce enormous amounts of raw energy. And it would certainly be advantageous for human beings to harness some of that energy, which could be converted to electricity to power homes, offices, public buildings, and even cars and ships. A number of scientists believe that such a goal will actually be attainable in the future. Admittedly, many difficult technical problems would have to be overcome before people could control and tap into these cosmic powerhouses. But after all, only a century ago space shuttles, artificial satellites, nuclear power, television, computers, and the Internet, all of which required the development of bold new technologies, did not exist.

Farming the energy of black holes would utilize the same basic principle used in existing types of energy production. Namely, when any kind of fuel is burned or destroyed, some of its mass is converted into energy, which people then exploit. When people burn oil or coal, only about 1 percent of the fuel's mass is converted into energy. Obviously, this is not very efficient and produces a lot of soot and other waste materials that pollute the environment. Even nuclear reactions, like those produced in nuclear power plants, convert only 2 or 3 percent of their mass into energy. By contrast, when matter is annihilated at the event horizon of a black hole, up to 30 percent of its mass becomes energy. In theory, people could stoke such a black hole furnace by firing asteroids and other space debris toward the hole, destroying the debris and thereby generating energy. If people could find a way to capture that energy, say by installing large collection grids around the hole, Earth could be provided with seemingly unlimited power.

On an even grander scale, given further technological advances, people might actually be able to create black holes from scratch. As John Taylor explains, this would yield mass-to-energy conversions considerably higher than 30 percent:

Hawking Radiation and Evaporating Black Holes

In 1974, English physicist Stephen Hawking surprised the scientific community by showing that black holes can give off radiation and thereby lose some of their mass. Some of the matter at the edge of the event horizon, he said, would consist of pairs of particles. One particle would be positively charged, the other negatively charged. In his book about Hawking, scholar Paul Strathern writes: "The black hole would attract the negative particle, while at the same time it would eject the positive particle. This would escape in the form of radiation." This radiation, now called Hawking radiation, would be in the form of heat. Its temperature would be "mere millionths of a degree above absolute zero," says Strathern, "but it would undeniably be there."

In his book *Explorations*, astronomer Thomas Arny points out that, because of this phenomenon, black holes must eventually evaporate. "However," he adds, "the time it takes for a solar-mass black hole to disappear by 'shining itself away' is *very* long—approximately 10^{67} years! This is . . . vastly larger than the age of the universe—but the implications are important: even black holes evolve and 'die.'"

We can envisage a technologically very advanced intelligent civilization which goes in for black-hole farming. To do this, they would spread hydrogen or helium throughout a region of a galaxy, or concentrate some already there, so that large stars were formed rapidly. These would then be used as energy generators during their nuclear burning phase, and allowed to collapse to black holes, also collecting supernova energy emitted during the short implosion [collapse] time. The resulting black holes would then be brought together in pairs by suitable methods to obtain a large fraction of their available energy. The resulting single black hole would then be finally exhausted of all its remaining available rotational and electrical energy. The amount of energy available in this way would be enormous.[28]

Of course, humans may never achieve the level of technology needed for such fantastic engineering projects. Also, they may find it too difficult and time-consuming to travel hundreds or thousands of light-years in search of stellar black holes to exploit. However, that does not necessarily rule out human exploitation of black hole–generated energy. A more modest and plausible approach would be to build instruments capable of detecting mini–black holes that stray through our solar system. Once found, such objects might be captured and mined in a manageable way. "A stream of frozen hydrogen pellets can . . . be aimed past the mini–black hole," says Asimov,

> so that it skims the Schwarzschild radius without entering it. Tidal [intense gravitational] effects will heat the hydrogen to the point of fusion, so that helium will come through at the other end. The mini–black hole will then prove the simplest and most foolproof nuclear reactor possible, and the energy it produces can be stored and sent down to Earth.[29]

These are only some of the ways in which the highly unusual properties of black holes may someday be exploited by humanity, or by other races of intelligent beings. Only time will tell.

Chapter 4

Detecting Black Holes Through Indirect Means

Long before scientists began dreaming about possibly capturing, controlling, and exploiting black holes for humanity's benefit, they dreamed of detecting and directly observing these cosmic oddities in the first place. Einstein, Schwarzschild, Kerr, and many others became certain that black holes *could* exist, but for a long time they could find no convincing evidence that they *do* exist.

The obvious problem in detecting black holes was that light's inability to escape them makes them appear black and invisible to human eyes and telescopes. And therefore, scientists could not confirm the existence of these objects by direct visual means. This forced them to resort to *in*direct means, mainly observations of the behavior of stars, gases, and other matter located near black holes. As it happened, however, the initial detection of black holes was not the result of a concerted effort to find these objects. It came instead as part of a process of elimination as astronomers attempted to explain the workings of some strange, and it turns out crucial, cosmic phenomena discovered in the second half of the twentieth century.

The X-Ray Universe

One of these important discoveries that eventually led to the detection of black holes was that the universe is virtually alive with X rays. These are an invisible form of electromagnetic radiation that is much more energetic and penetrating than visible light. First discovered in laboratory experiments in 1895 by German physicist Wilhelm Roentgen, X rays are familiar to most people from their use in medicine. When a technician aims a beam of X rays at the human body, most of the rays pass through the body and strike a photographic plate, which renders a ghostly image of the patient's insides.

The bright patches in this X-ray image of the Sun's outer atmosphere, or corona, are X-rays emitted from extremely hot gases.

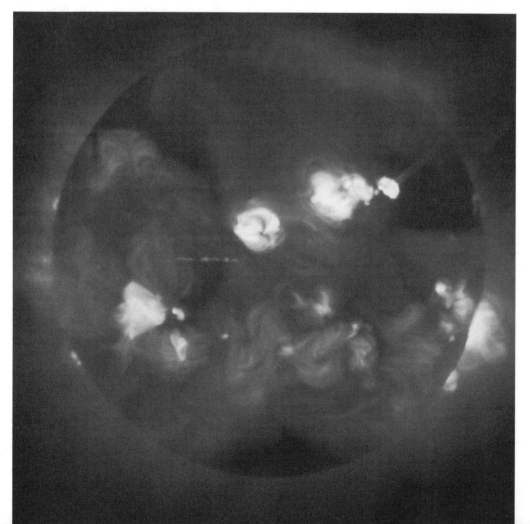

In the years that followed Roentgen's discovery, as artificially produced X rays became increasingly common medical tools, a few astronomers began to suspect that the Sun might produce this energetic radiation naturally. But they had no inkling of the virtual sea of X rays originating from beyond our star. As Herbert Friedman puts it, "There was no hint of the enormous portent [clue or foreshadowing] for the future of astronomy. Astronomers remained oblivious to the potential of X-ray astronomy."[30]

The first confirmation that the Sun does indeed produce X rays came in 1948, when American scientists attached detection instruments to rockets developed by the Germans in World War II. Although the instruments did detect solar X rays, they showed that the Sun is not a strong X-ray source; the volume of X rays it produces is only about one-millionth that of the visible light it emits. Thus, it appeared to scientists that stars in general would not prove to be important sources of X rays.

Then, in June 1962, American scientists launched a rocket carrying instruments designed to detect possible radiation coming from the surface of the Moon. The experiment found no radiation on the

Launched in July 1999, the Chandra X-ray Observatory has discovered thousands of previously unknown X-ray sources.

Moon. But it did quite unexpectedly detect a powerful X-ray source located beyond the solar system. Later rocket launches confirmed the existence of this source and pinpointed it in the constellation of Scorpius, the scorpion. Astronomers named it Scorpius X-1, or Sco X-1 for short.

After that, other distant, very powerful X-ray sources were discovered, especially following the December 1970 launch of a more sophisticated X-ray satellite. This device, named Uhuru, and several even more sensitive probes launched later, revealed that the sky is literally filled with X-ray sources; some scientists began to refer to this previously unknown phenomenon as the "X-ray universe."

A Black Hole's Presence Revealed

It soon became clear to astronomers that Sco X-1 and many similar strong X-ray sources, including the pulsar in the Crab Nebula, are neutron stars. And they were able to develop a model to explain how neutron stars that are part of binary star systems can emit strong bursts of X rays. John Gribbin explains that in a binary star system, the two objects, one a normal star and the other a small superdense neutron star, are

> orbiting each other, locked in a mutual gravitational embrace. . . . Gas from the atmosphere of the large star will be torn away from it by tidal effects and attracted to the small star. As the gas spirals down onto the small star, it will form a swirling disk of material, generating heat within the disk itself. . . . The small, dense star is surrounded by very hot gas, or plasma, which radiates at X-ray wavelengths . . . and is constantly being renewed by gas falling in from the larger star.[31]

The fact that these strong X-ray sources are neutron stars indicated to astronomers that large bursts of X rays are often associated with superdense cosmic bodies. Considering this, at least a few scientists could not help but suspect that another kind of superdense object—the then hypothetical black hole—might somehow reveal its presence by producing X rays. And indeed, one strong X-ray source first detected in the 1960s did seem to be a promising black hole candidate. Located in the constellation of Cygnus, the swan, it became known as Cygnus X-l, or Cyg X-1 for short.

Like Sco X-l, Cyg X-1 is part of a binary star system. But unlike the case of Sco X-l, the object orbiting the normal star in the Cyg X-1 system emits no visible light at all. Also, the bursts of X rays coming from Cyg X-1 occur at astonishing rates—as high as a thousand or more per second. This tells astronomers that the invisible object must be extremely small and compact. According to Friedman (who in the 1960s boldly predicted that Sco X-1 was a neutron star):

> A star cannot change its brightness in less time than it takes light [or X rays and other forms of electromagnetic radiation] to cross its diameter. . . . Thus, when Cyg X-1 exhibited millisecond bursts, it meant that the X-ray-emitting region could be no more than 300 kilometers [about 186 miles] across.[32]

Another reason why scientists suspected that the Cyg X-1 object is a black hole is that it is tremendously massive for such a tiny body. The normal star in the system is a giant of about thirty solar masses. Astronomers were able to work out its orbital characteristics and from this calculate the mass of the invisible companion. They found it to be nine solar masses, too massive to be a neutron star, which strongly suggested that the Cyg X-1 system harbors a stellar black hole.

It is now clear that Cyg X-1 emits such strong bursts of X rays through a combination of the black

hole's powerful gravity and its close proximity to the larger companion star. The black hole is a bit closer to the other star than the planet Mercury is to the Sun. (Mercury lies about 36 million miles from the Sun.) Such extremely close quarters for these massive bodies allow the black hole's gravity to draw gases from the outer layers of the companion. As these gases spiral in toward the denser object, they form a huge, rapidly spinning, and very hot accretion disk around the outside of the hole's event horizon. Slowly but surely, some of the gases are pulled right up to the horizon, where the hole's immense gravity tears the gases' atoms apart. This extremely violent process releases strong bursts of X rays only an instant before the stream of matter disappears forever beyond the event horizon. In the minutes, days, and years that follow, the X rays emitted in this manner travel outward, eventually reaching Earth and showing scientists the position of the black hole.

An artist's view of what the Cygnus X-1 system may look like. Matter from the giant star is drawn away into the black hole's accretion disk.

The Mystery of Gamma-Ray Bursts

Black holes likely also reveal their presence by generating powerful bursts of gamma rays. Even more energetic than X rays, gamma rays are in fact the most energetic and penetrating kind of radiation in the electromagnetic spectrum. Like X rays, in high enough doses gamma rays can be lethal to living things; that is why doctors sometimes use small, controlled doses of gamma rays to destroy cancerous tumors.

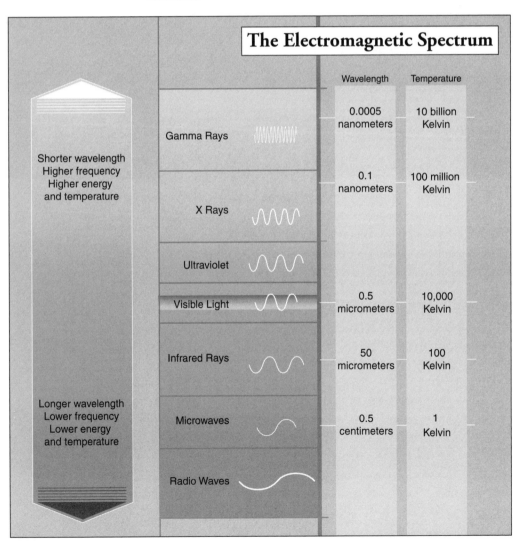

The Electromagnetic Spectrum

	Wavelength	Temperature
Gamma Rays	0.0005 nanometers	10 billion Kelvin
X Rays	0.1 nanometers	100 million Kelvin
Ultraviolet		
Visible Light	0.5 micrometers	10,000 Kelvin
Infrared Rays	50 micrometers	100 Kelvin
Microwaves	0.5 centimeters	1 Kelvin
Radio Waves		

Shorter wavelength
Higher frequency
Higher energy
and temperature

Longer wavelength
Lower frequency
Lower energy
and temperature

Also like X rays, gamma rays captured the attention of astronomers in the 1960s. Detectors mounted on American rockets began to record strange, very powerful bursts of gamma rays coming from random parts of the sky. Typical bursts lasted a few seconds, although some flared up and then diminished in less than a second. Because nuclear explosions emit brief bursts of gamma rays, at first American scientists and security personnel worried that the Soviet Union might be conducting secret nuclear tests beyond Earth's atmosphere.

By 1973, however, scientists had become convinced that the gamma-ray bursts (or GRBs) are a naturally occurring phenomenon originating deep in space. A new burst was detected at least once a week on average. Although the GRBs varied in intensity, some were truly enormous, in the range of a billion trillion times the luminosity of the Sun. Put another way, a big GRB releases as much energy in 10 seconds as the Sun does in 10 billion years. Astronomers were very hard pressed to explain what could be causing these huge cosmic outbursts. From 1973 to 1991, the prevailing theory was that GRBs were telltale signs of "star quakes" (similar to earthquakes) on neutron stars; some thought that perhaps a wayward planet crashing into a neutron star releases a sudden burst of gamma rays.

In recent years, however, astronomers have concluded that the physical attributes of gamma-ray bursts are better explained as by-products of the workings of large black holes. Several different scenarios have been suggested; any one of them, and indeed perhaps all of them, may be occurring at intervals not only in our own galaxy, the Milky Way, but also in the billions of other galaxies lying beyond it.

One recent hypothesis, advanced by MIT scientist Maurice Van Putten, suggests that in binary star systems containing a normal star and a black hole, the

When Black Holes Merge

Strong evidence that black holes do sometimes collide and merge was recently discovered by David Merritt, of Rutgers University, and Ronald Ekers, of the Australia Telescope National Facility. They studied patterns of radio waves given off by a group of distant galaxies. One strange feature that these galaxies have in common is a curious X-shaped structure at their centers. Merritt and Ekers believe that the four lobes making up such an X are high-speed jets of material emitted from a black hole that has recently merged with another black hole. In this view, the violence of the merger knocks the new black hole off its axis, and for a while it emits two sets of jets, one from its previous alignment, the other from its new alignment.

In an interview by Vanessa Thomas in the November 2002 issue of *Astronomy*, Merritt says, "Black holes are so large and massive, the only thing we can imagine that would have enough force to realign them is another black hole. . . . [Before this discovery] most astronomers were fairly sure that black holes coalesce, but we now regard the X-shaped galaxies as the first 'smoking-gun' evidence."

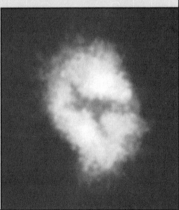

The X-shaped structure in this gaseous cloud may be evidence of two black holes merging.

black hole eventually siphons off nearly all of the companion star's material. Finally, all that is left of the normal star is a doughnut-shaped ring that becomes part of the hole's spinning accretion disk. In the span of only a few seconds, the hole sucks in the remaining pieces of the companion, in the process creating an enormous outburst of gamma rays.

In another scenario, a large GRB is generated when a stellar black hole collides with either a neutron star or another black hole. In either case, the colliding bodies would merge as one, releasing an immense burst of energy. "The two stars spiral together," Begelman and Rees speculate, slowly at first and then faster and faster, until they finally merge. The final coalescence, perhaps lasting only a millisecond, would certainly trigger a large enough release of energy. Such events are rare—they would occur only once every 100,000 years in a typical galaxy. But there are at least a billion galaxies within [effective range of human detectors], so the rate at which bursts are detected [about one per day by the late 1990s] poses no real problem.[33]

In still another model for black holes and GRBs, a large gamma-ray burst occurs when people on Earth witness the birth of a stellar black hole from a specific and favorable angle. In this view, the tremendous collapse of a giant star into a black hole produces more than a supernova and a superdense object. The implosion also generates an enormous outpouring of gamma rays from the collapsing object's poles. Because the alignment of such objects in the universe is random, only rarely will one's poles point directly at Earth. When they do not line up, humans see only the bright flash of the supernova; but when the object's poles *are* aligned with Earth, human instruments record a giant outburst of gamma rays as well as the supernova.

Solving the Riddle of Quasars

Gamma-ray bursts are not the only cosmic mystery that astronomers have attempted to solve by invoking the bizarre properties and effects of black holes. In 1963, an extremely strange object was discovered in the constellation of Virgo, the virgin. Dubbed 3C 273, the object is situated at the enormous distance of 2 billion light-years from our solar system. (This means that it takes light and other radiation emitted by the object 2 billion years to reach us!) Astronomers noted that 3C 273 gives off both visible light and strong jets of radio waves and other kinds of electromagnetic radiation. What made the object seem so unusual was that this outpouring energy is hundreds of times greater than that of the entire Milky Way galaxy, which is made up of billions of stars; yet 3C 273 appeared to be extremely small—the size of a single star. Thus, the bizarre object and others like it discovered in the years that followed looked something like stars. But they were obviously not ordinary stars. So astronomers called them quasi-stellar ("starlike") objects, or quasars for short. By 2003 some thirteen thousand quasars had been found; and experts estimate that as many as ninety thousand more will be discovered in the next couple of decades.

At first, astronomers had no credible idea of what could be causing quasars to shine so brightly. Nor did they think to connect them with black holes, which in the early 1960s were still viewed as fascinating but mainly hypothetical constructs. As time went on, however, careful observations of quasars revealed certain exotic characteristics increasingly associated with superdense bodies. In the words of University of Alabama astronomer William C. Keel:

> Despite shining far brighter than ordinary galaxies, quasars change brightness on short timescales. Indeed, their X-ray output can vary in *minutes*. . . . This shows that most of the radiation must come from tiny regions, maybe no more than light-hours across, or roughly the orbit diameter of Uranus or Neptune. Along with their small size, quasars must have central engines with gravitational fields strong enough to hold onto gas that's moving at thousands of kilometers per second. Also, the gas must be exposed to high temperatures or energetic radiation to create the observed . . . [amount of] X-ray emission. Finally, the extent and speed of the radio-emitting jets show that the source has a directional memory [i.e., always emits the jets in the same direction] and can eject material so

close to the speed of light that it escapes in spectacular fashion. So what kind of an object can do all this? The most reasonable explanation is an enormous black hole.[34]

A quasar-producing black hole gives off a tremendous outburst of energy in much the same way that

Twinkle, Twinkle Quasi-Star

For a number of years scientists viewed quasars as weird and mysterious objects that did not seem to belong in the "normal" universe. This air of mystery was captured perfectly in 1964 by renowned Russian-born American physicist George Gamow (1904–1968) in a short poem titled "Quasar" (which has since that time been reproduced in hundreds of books and articles about black holes, quasars, and other cosmic oddities).

Twinkle, twinkle, quasi-star
Biggest puzzle from afar
How unlike the other ones
Brighter than a billion suns
Twinkle, twinkle, quasi-star
How I wonder what you are.

This bright quasar with a long X-ray jet lies 10 billion light-years away.

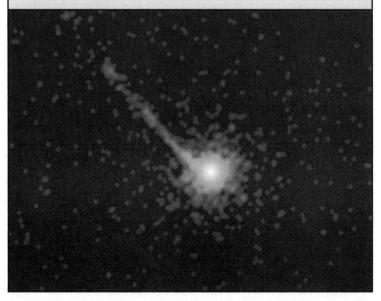

an ordinary stellar black hole reveals itself by an X-ray signature. In the latter situation, matter from the accretion disk that is about to cross the event horizon is annihilated, releasing powerful bursts of X rays. Astronomer Mark A. Garlick describes the similar process involved in quasar formation:

> Most astronomers are now convinced that a vast accretion disk of gas and dust, the gravitationally shredded remains of countless stars and nebulae [cosmic gas clouds], surrounds the black hole in a quasar. As the gas in the disk spirals toward the black hole's deadly maw, the material becomes so compressed and heated that it generates the truly enormous quantities of light that make quasars conspicuous across billions of light-years.[35]

What, then, makes a quasar-producing black hole different from an ordinary stellar black hole? Keel and Garlick hint at the answer in their use of the phrases "enormous black hole" and "vast accretion disk." Only a black hole that has acquired a gigantic mass—equal to that of millions or even billions of stars—could produce the spectacular celestial fireworks called quasars. The notion that such objects could actually exist was eye-opening enough for scientists. But even more intriguing was the fact that quasars are always located in the centers of galaxies. From this realization, it was only a minor leap to the startling suggestion that gigantic black holes might exist in the hearts of *all* galaxies.

Chapter 5

Giant Black Holes and the Fate of the Universe

As long as stellar black holes were the only kind of black holes for which science could find even indirect evidence, the universe seemed a far less scary place than it does today. After all, stellar black holes did not appear to pose any major short- or long-term danger to the universe as a whole or to the existence of life within it. True, when a giant star collapses to form a black hole, any living things inhabiting the planets or moons of that solar system will first be fried and then frozen. No life of any kind will be able to survive for very long. However, these lethal effects would remain localized to that system. This is because the distances separating most stars are immense—about four to seven light-years, or 24 trillion to 42 trillion miles. The gravitational effects and radiation of even the most massive stellar black hole could be felt over only a small fraction of such distances. Therefore, this kind of black hole would pose no credible threat to neighboring stars, their planets, and any life forms they might harbor.

When one considers the larger scheme of things, however, such safety zones become illusory and ultimately useless. Scientists now know that the danger posed by black holes increases significantly in areas of space where many large stars lie very close together (on the order of only a few light-weeks, light-days, or even light-hours apart). In such an environment, several neighboring giant stars can collapse into black holes over time. As these superdense objects drift and meander, some will merge, producing more massive bodies with stronger gravities.

This drawing depicts a black hole wreaking havoc at the center of a galaxy. Most or all galaxies may harbor such objects.

Finally, one very massive black hole will dominate the scene. It will continue to draw in clouds of gas, stars, planets, smaller black holes, and other materials floating in its cluttered cosmic neighborhood; and over the course of millions and billions of years, it will grow still more massive. Indeed, it will become a sort of cosmic monster with an insatiable appetite. Only recently have astronomers come to the unsettling realization that such giant, or supermassive, black holes not only exist, they may well play a major role in the ongoing evolution and ultimate fate of the universe and everything in it.

Midsized Black Holes

First, it is important to determine just how massive a black hole must be to qualify as a giant. The standard stellar black holes that scientists believe exist in some binary star systems are mostly in the range of about eight to twenty, and occasionally up to about fifty, solar masses. By earthly and human standards, these are very massive objects to be sure. But in the last few years, evidence has been found for the existence of much more substantial black holes.

These larger black holes fall into two broad categories—intermediate, or midsized, holes, and supermassive, or giant, holes. Since the early 1970s, astronomers had speculated about the possibility of midsized black holes, which they theorized would contain from a few hundred to several tens of thousands of solar masses. It was clear that such objects would most likely form in regions of densely packed stars and gas clouds; after all, the holes would have to have a lot of matter to feed on to grow so large. One such crowded region is a globular cluster, of which the Milky Way contains several hundred. Isaac Asimov describes globular clusters as stellar groups in which

> some tens of thousands or even hundreds of thousands of stars are clustered together in a well-packed sphere. Here in our own neighborhood of the universe, stars are separated by an average distance of about 5 light-years. At the center of a globular cluster, they may be separated by an average distance of ½ light-year. A given volume of space in a globular cluster might include 1,000 times as many stars as that same volume in our own neighborhood.[36]

Astronomers examined several globular clusters in the 1970s and found that they did emit high doses of X rays, as the likely black hole candidate Cyg X-1 did. However, no concrete evidence for midsized black holes in these star groups surfaced until 2002. Late that year, a team led by Roeland Van Der Marel at the Space Telescope Institute found two midsized black holes. One, possessing about four thousand solar masses, is in M15, a globular cluster in the Milky Way. The other resides in G1, a globular cluster in the neighboring Andromeda galaxy, and has roughly twenty thousand solar masses. In an interview following the

The globular cluster M15, located about thirty-three thousand light-years away in the constellation Pegasus, appears to have a large black hole in its center.

discovery, Luis Ho, one of the team members, exclaimed: "It's very exciting to finally find compelling evidence that nature knows how to make these strange beasts."[37]

Early in 2003, another research team, this one led by Jon Miller at the Harvard-Smithsonian Center for Astrophysics, discovered two more midsized black holes. Situated in a spiral galaxy designated NGC 1313, lying at a distance of 10 million light-years from Earth, they each contain several hundred solar masses.

Something Frightening in the Core

Proof for the existence of members of the other broad category of larger-than-stellar black holes—the supermassive ones—has also begun to emerge in recent years. These giants always appear to inhabit the centers, or cores, of galaxies, so it has become common to refer to them as "galactic black holes." The reasons that it took so long to verify their existence are fairly simple. First, the cores of galaxies are extremely far away; even the center of our own Milky Way lies at the considerable distance of about twenty-six thousand light-years. Second, the galactic cores are also generally blocked from easy viewing by dense layers of gases, dust, and other cosmic debris.

In spite of these obstacles, astronomers persevered. Over the years, new and larger telescopes, along with more sophisticated detection equipment, revealed more and more information about the Milky Way's core. There, it became clear, many huge stars lie very close together. Some of them are as large as 120 or more times the size of the Sun, and many of them float among the expanding and often overlapping gaseous remnants of many prior supernovas. "Like silken drapes blown in the wind," writes noted science writer Robert Zimmerman,

A Hubble Space Telescope photo of the galaxy NGC 4414. Both it and the Milky Way, which it resembles, likely contain giant black holes.

> the erupting waves of gas from scores of supernovas sweep through an inner region approximately 350 light-years across, filling space like froth and geysers. Here supergiant stars—many times more massive than the sun and rare elsewhere in the galaxy—number in the hundreds.

And within those 350 light-years are three of the galaxy's densest and most massive star clusters, surrounded by millions of additional stars. So packed is this core that if the solar system were located there, a handful of stars [in addition to the sun] would float among the planets.[38]

More ominously, astronomers also discovered something dark, monstrous, and frightening in the crowded galactic core. Almost all stars and other matter there are sweeping very rapidly around an extremely massive object. The first hints that something unusual lay in the center of our galaxy came in the 1950s. Radio telescopes, huge bowl-shaped antennas that gather and record radio waves from outer space, showed that a powerful source of these waves lies in the galactic core. These early images were crude and inconclusive. And thanks to the masses of gases and dust obscuring the core, visual images showed nothing.

Imitating Master Yoda

It took the development of more advanced radio telescopes in ensuing decades to begin to unravel the mystery of the Milky Way's core. In the mid-1970s, radio images revealed three distinct nonstellar objects in the core. Two, which looked like hazy, cloudlike patches, were dubbed Sagittarius East and Sagittarius West (after Sagittarius, the archer, the constellation in which the core is situated in Earth's night sky). The third object, a pointlike, very powerful radio-wave source lying in the galaxy's very center, received the name Sagittarius A* (pronounced A-star).

For a long time, astronomers were puzzled by Sagittarius A*. It is clearly too energetic and hot to be an ordinary star. Indeed, studies reveal that it is hotter than any other object in the Milky Way. In the 1980s and early 1990s, more sophisticated images of the core were taken using infrared telescopes, which can see through most of the layers of gases and dust.

These showed huge filaments of gases swirling around Sagittarius A*. Even more detail was revealed in 1997 by German astronomers Andrea Eckart and Reinhard Genzel, who announced that they had mapped the frenzied motions of the seventy stars closest to the core's central object. According to Zimmerman:

> They found that many of the stars were streaking across the sky at tremendous speeds, and that the closer to Sagittarius A* the stars were, the faster they moved. Stars at distances of more than half a light-year traveled at less than 100 miles per second. Closer in, the speeds increased to more than 500 miles per second, and the closest star to Sagittarius A*, dubbed S1, also had the fastest velocity, estimated at almost 900 miles per second. Furthermore, Eckart and Genzel found that the 100 nearest stars seemed to be moving in a generally clockwise direction, opposite to the rotation of the rest of the galaxy. This suggests that they were part of a large torus [doughnut-shaped structure] of stars orbiting a single invisible point. At the center of this whirling collection of stars was the radio source Sagittarius A*, which unlike any other star in the sky has no apparent proper [visible] motion.[39]

Members of the scientific community are now nearly unanimous in their belief that Sagittarius A* is a supermassive black hole. As for just how massive it is, numerous estimates appeared in the 1990s, the most common being 2.6 million solar masses. In October 2002, however, the results of a study by Rainer Schödel, of Germany's Max Planck Institute for Extraterrestrial Physics, showed a larger mass for the giant black hole—3.7 million times that of the Sun.

To measure the mass of Sagittarius A*, the scientists observed the speeds at which matter is orbiting it and determined how massive the central object would have to be to produce these movements. "In the same way that Master Yoda and his disciples [in the *Star Wars* series] saw through an attempt to wipe a planet from the Jedi archives [by detecting the telltale signs of the planet's gravity]," William Keel quips, "astronomers can discern the existence of this object."[40]

The Chicken or the Egg?

Having already drawn in and consumed more than 3 million stars, Sagittarius A* is certainly far more massive than stellar and midsized black holes (not to mention mini–black holes). Yet mounting evidence suggests that this giant's growth cycle is far from finished. As Keel points out, "Even at a mass of 3 million suns, this black hole proves quite modest by the standards of other galaxies."[41]

Indeed, astronomers have intensified their studies of galactic cores and continue to discover truly enormous supermassive black holes in many distant galaxies. The nearby Andromeda galaxy, for instance, harbors a 30-million-solar-mass black hole in its core. A galaxy named NGC 4486B has a central black hole measuring about 500 million solar masses, and the core of a galaxy designated NGC 4261 features a stupendous object of some 1.2 billion solar masses. This suggests that there may be no physical limit to the size of a supermassive black hole.

Also, the fact that these giants seem to be integral features of galaxies and that they are eating their way through the galactic cores is surely significant. It now appears certain that supermassive galactic black holes must strongly affect the structure, evolution, and ultimate fate of galaxies. Says science writer Steve Nadis, "New evidence strongly suggests a much more intimate connection than astronomers ever thought possible between galaxies and the supermassive black holes that dominate their cores."[42]

But the nature of this grand cosmic connection is for the moment problematic for scientists. Central to

Sagittarius A* Rips a Star Apart

In this excerpt from an article in the October 2001 issue of *Astronomy* magazine, science writer Robert Zimmerman describes the possible origins of Sagittarius East. It is now believed to be the remnants of an unusual supernova created by the immense gravitational effects of the black hole Sagittarius A*.

Sagittarius East is now believed to be a large bubble, possibly one of the largest supernova remnants known, that formed fewer than 100,000 years ago and maybe as recently as 10,000 years ago. Although it engulfs Sagittarius West [a cloudlike region nearby] and Sagittarius A*, it lies mostly behind both. Astronomers think that the energy required to punch out this shell of gas in such a dense region would have to be as much as 50 times greater than the most powerful supernova explosion. What could have produced this much energy still puzzles astronomers. Some theorize that Sagittarius East was created when a star approached within 50 million miles of the central black hole and was torn apart by the strong gravity.

At the center of this mass of gaseous clouds lies Sagittarius A*, which astronomers believe to be a giant black hole.

the present debate on the topic is a variation of the old "chicken or the egg" question, in this case, Which came first, galaxies or giant black holes? Some astronomers think that galaxies and their central black holes form from the "outside in." In other words, swirling masses of gases and dust condense to form spinning galaxies of stars, and over time some of the giant stars in the core collapse into black holes, which in turn merge to become one really massive black hole.

In contrast, others argue for the "inside out" hypothesis. In this version, as Asimov says, "The black hole may have come first and then served as a 'seed,' gathering stars about itself as super-accretion disks that become clusters and galaxies."[43] As for where these initial seed black holes came from, no one knows. They may have been created somehow in the Big Bang along with mini–black holes.

Whichever came first—galaxies or large black holes—the two seem to grow and develop together in step, so to speak. Late in 2000, astronomer Michael Merrifield and his colleagues at the University of Nottingham, in England, found a telling correlation between the age of galaxies and the masses of the supermassive black holes at their cores. Simply put, the older the galaxy, the more massive its central hole. "We're measuring the time scale over which black holes grow," Merrifield explains, "and it appears to be comparable to the age of the host galaxies. So they really are developing together."[44]

This new finding raises an important question. If giant black holes continue to grow at the expense of their host galaxies, why do astronomers not see some galaxies in their death throes, almost totally absorbed by the cosmic monsters within? The most obvious answer is that the universe is not yet old enough. Indeed, present-day humans probably exist at a time in the life cycle of the universe when most galactic black holes are still relative youngsters pos-

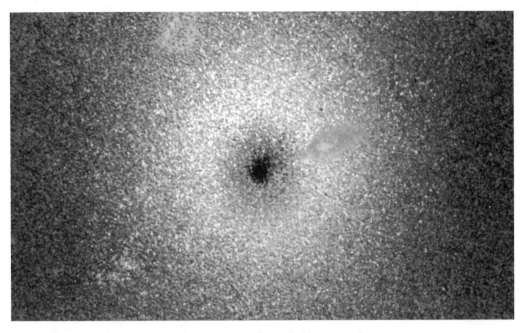

sessing from a few million to a few billion solar masses. According to this view, if humans could somehow travel far ahead in time, they would see many galactic black holes with tens and hundreds of billions of solar masses devouring the last remains of their parent galaxies.

Stars in the center of the galaxy called M87 are tightly packed and moving very fast, suggesting they are orbiting a massive black hole.

The Oscillating Universe

If this scenario is correct, what does the awesome process of giant black holes consuming entire galaxies mean for the future of the universe and for humans and any other intelligent beings that may exist in the vast reaches of space? First, the process will take a long time, perhaps thirty, fifty, or even hundreds of billions of years or more. So most galaxies and intelligent civilizations are not in any immediate danger. Eventually, though, Sagittarius A* will likely swallow up all the normal matter surrounding it, including the Sun and its planets. After its humongous meal, this bloated black hole may then float through space until it encounters other giant holes that have already devoured their own former galaxies. And relentless gravity will inevitably cause these phenomenally massive objects to move ever closer to one another and merge in an embrace of self-annihilation.

Carrying this possible sequence of future events even further, after unknown numbers of eons all of the galactic black holes—together containing all the former matter in the universe—might merge into one huge monster of a black hole. The fate of this bizarre cosmic creature can only be guessed. But some astronomers postulate that this ultimate end of the present universe will somehow give rise to the birth of a new one. Perhaps there will be a new Big Bang, in which immense quantities of matter rush outward from a central point and slowly coalesce into stars, galaxies, planets, and so forth. Logically, in this new universe new black holes will form. And

Searching for a Definite Beginning

In this excerpt from his book *Black Holes*, scientist John Taylor points out that the concept that the present universe developed from a black hole containing the remnants of a prior universe is difficult for humans to comprehend because it does not define the beginning of the process.

The hardest question of all to answer is where did our universe come from? If we reply that it came from somewhere else, brought to its present state by the laws of physics, we need only add that somewhere else, filled with whatever was in it before it formed us and our material surroundings, to our present world. We then ask again, where did that new totality come from? Any definite answer to our first question is the wrong one, since it would lead us to an infinite chain of similar questions. . . . But we could try to find from what our world, as we know it today, arose. We might do so by conjecturing that our present universe sprang into being from the final stage of collapse in a spinning black hole in a different universe, bubbling out of the black hole's center. . . . That might or might not fit with experimental facts if we looked for them carefully enough, but it would still beg the question, since we would then have to explain where the previous universe came from.

in time, these will slowly but steadily begin a new cycle of growth and merger. Astronomers call this theoretical situation in which all matter repeatedly contracts and rebounds the "oscillating universe."

It is only natural to wonder about what will happen to humanity in the ultimate cosmic crunch, when all matter in the present universe is incorporated into one or more titanic black holes. However, it is highly unlikely that human beings, at least in their present form, will exist billions of years from now. If our species is not long since extinct by that time, it will have undergone profound physical and mental changes, enough to be totally unrecognizable to people alive today. Still, it is at least possible that our descendants, in whatever form, will be around to witness the climactic ending of what will become essentially an all-black-hole universe. Could they survive the final crunch? John Taylor gives this thought-provoking answer:

> The fate of the physical universe is catastrophic. . . . It is either to be crushed into its fundamental constituents, as far as possible, to make a universal black hole, or it is to be slowly absorbed by local black holes, again to be crushed out of existence as we know it. . . . At such an end, [we would surely face physical death, so] we could only appeal to our souls, if they exist, to preserve us. . . . It could only be if the universe bounces back again after its collapse that these separated souls have any chance of returning. . . . There is very little evidence of such a bounce being able to occur, but if it does, only then can one expect any form of immortality.[45]

Chapter 6

Can Black Holes Be Used as Cosmic Gateways?

So far, stellar and galactic black holes have been considered in light of how their major properties—extreme gravity, accretion disks, quasars, and so forth—affect matter, space, and time in the universe surrounding them. Very little has been said about what happens inside a black hole other than that matter is either crushed or falls down the hole's gravity well forever. This is partly because the inner workings of these cosmic oddities remain largely mysterious. Obviously, there is no known way to see into or directly measure the inside of a black hole.

But that has certainly not stopped people from trying to visualize what lies beyond the enigmatic event horizon. Ever since serious consideration of black holes began in the 1960s, various theories and mathematical equations have predicted that certain things are likely to exist or occur inside black holes. And when the theories have seemed inadequate, investigators have freely used their imaginations. They have wondered, for example, whether bodies outside the hole would be visible from the inside since they know that matter inside a black hole is not visible from the outside. Also, matter that enters a black hole disappears from the regular universe. Does this matter cease to exist, or does it somehow survive and reemerge somewhere else, either in this universe or another one? Moreover, if the matter *can* survive intact, might it be possible for people, too, to survive a trip into a black hole?

Not surprisingly, science fiction writers have frequently and colorfully exploited these and other bizarre possible qualities of the inner environments of black holes. Most often, they portray these superdense objects disturbing the fabric of space and finally tearing it, thereby creating a small opening. Such an opening and the invisible spatial tunnel it leads to are together commonly referred to as a wormhole. As of yet, wormholes are technically theoretical, although physicists believe they are likely to exist.

Science fiction stories and films usually describe piloted spacecraft traveling through wormholes and emerging either in distant regions of the galaxy or in the past or future. In the popular television series

Wormholes as Time Machines

Some of the mathematical formulas associated with the theory of wormholes suggest that if one end of a hole is fixed and the other end is moving, each will end in a different time frame. In this excerpt from *The Physics of Star Trek*, physicist Lawrence M. Krauss tells how writers for *Star Trek: Voyager* correctly depicted this phenomenon.

Wormholes, as glorious as they would be for tunneling through vast distances in space, have an even more remarkable potential, glimpsed most recently in the *Voyager* episode "Eye of the Needle." In this episode, the *Voyager* crew discovered a small wormhole leading back to their own "alpha quadrant" of the galaxy. After communicating through it, they found to their horror that it led not to the alpha quadrant they knew and loved but to the alpha quadrant of a generation earlier. The two ends of the wormhole connected space at two different times! Well, this is another one of those instances in which the *Voyager* writers got it right. If wormholes exist, they can well be time machines! This startling realization has grown over the last decade, as various theorists . . . began to investigate the physics of wormholes a little more seriously.

Babylon 5, for example, an interstellar space station floats near wormholes leading to various distant star systems. And in the final episode of the television series *Star Trek: Voyager*, Captain Janeway uses a wormhole to travel through both space and time in an effort to alter the past. Incredibly, in recent years physicists have shown that these kinds of journeys, though certainly not feasible using existing human technology, are theoretically possible.

Envisioning Hyperspace

Indeed, noted planetary scientist Carl Sagan learned of this possibility to his delight in the summer of 1985. At the time, he was working on a science fiction novel titled *Contact* and wanted his main character to traverse huge cosmic distances in very short time spans in a scientifically plausible way. Not being a specialist in general relativity, Sagan turned to one of the leading experts in that field, Kip Thorne, of the California Institute of Technology (or Caltech for short). "It occurred to me," Thorne later wrote, "that his novel could serve as a . . . tool for students studying general relativity."[46] With this in mind, Thorne accepted the challenge and enlisted the aid of two of his doctoral students, Michael Morris and Ulvi Yurtsever.

After exploring the mathematical possibilities, they informed Sagan that a spacetime geometry incorporating the concept of wormholes as cosmic gateways was theoretically possible. One gateway might allow matter to enter "hyperspace," a hypothetical region lying beyond normal space, and exit back into space

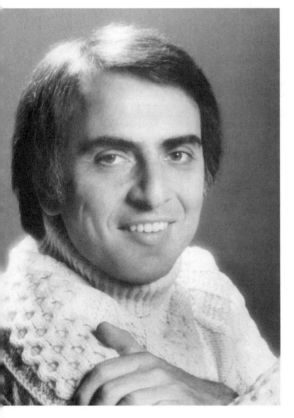

The late astronomer, planetary scientist, and author Carl Sagan depicted space travel via wormholes in his popular novel Contact.

at another similar portal. "To be sure," John Gribbin points out,

> the physical requirements appear contrived and implausible. But that isn't the point. What matters is that there seems to be nothing in the laws of physics that forbids travel through wormholes. The science-fiction writers were right—hyperspace connections do, at least in theory, provide a means to travel to distant regions of the universe without spending thousands of years puttering along through ordinary flat space at less than the speed of light.[47]

Sagan's inquiry and the Caltech team's calculations stimulated a sudden burst of interest in the scientific community. And since that time a good deal of research into wormholes and possible travel through them has been conducted. These efforts did not come out of a scientific vacuum, however. Decades before, a few scientists had considered the basic idea that wormholes might be a physical consequence of the warping of space by black holes. In 1916, shortly after Einstein's and Schwarzschild's equations for general relativity appeared, an Austrian scientist, Ludwig Flamm, examined them closely. Flamm pointed out that these equations allowed for some kind of invisible connection between two distinct regions of spacetime. German mathematician Hermann Weyl came to a similar conclusion in the 1920s.

In 1935, Einstein himself, working with a colleague, Nathan Rosen, explored the concept of this mysterious connection in more detail, including its relation to superdense objects. They conjectured that a sort of tunnel might exist inside a black hole. This tunnel, which would inhabit a region outside of normal space, might connect with another black hole somewhere else. For a while, researchers called such cosmic tunnels Einstein-Rosen bridges, after the men who first proposed them; only later did they acquire the name wormholes.

A World Turned Upside Down?

It should be emphasized that Einstein and Rosen did not mean to suggest that people could actually enter a black hole and use it as a gateway to somewhere else. They merely showed that mathematics did not forbid the existence of such tunnels. They did not pretend to know how big, how long, or how safe these tunnels might be, and in any case, the idea of traveling though them seemed irrelevant. For one thing, mathematical calculations indicated that any such wormhole would open up for no more than 1/10,000 of a second and then close. Indeed, it would not stay open long enough to allow even light to travel from one end of the tunnel to the other, so how could a much slower-moving space-ship get through? Also, all of these scientists agreed that any matter entering a black hole, including a person, would be demolished; even his or her atoms would be torn apart. So no space traveler who did fly into a black hole would survive long enough to make it to the wormhole, let alone travel through it.

However, in the 1960s new research began to alter this seemingly hopeless outlook. Flamm, Einstein, Rosen, and the others had based their calculations and opinions mainly on the workings of static, non-spinning Schwarzschild black holes. Yet as time went on, more and more scientists agreed that such bodies are theoretical constructs and do not exist in the real universe. When Roy Kerr introduced his mathematical solution for spinning black holes and it became clear that all such superdense bodies must be rotating, the picture of a black hole's interior changed. Now it could be seen that the singularity is shaped like a ring rather than an infinitely tiny point. And the mathematics for such rotating rings does suggest that matter can pass through them without being

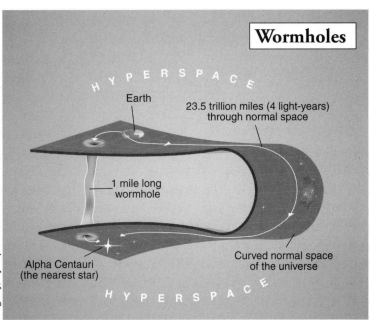

Source: *Black Holes and Time Warps: Einstein's Outrageous Legacy*, by Kip S. Thorne. New York: W.W. Norton, 1994.

Wormholes

HYPERSPACE

Earth

23.5 trillion miles (4 light-years) through normal space

1 mile long wormhole

Alpha Centauri (the nearest star)

Curved normal space of the universe

HYPERSPACE

crushed. (Of course, this does not rule out the possibility that the matter will suffer other lethal effects, such as bombardment by deadly radiation.)

The idea that a ring singularity might be a portal to a wormhole in hyperspace opens up a host of intriguing possibilities for the geometry of the region inside a black hole. Among these is the notion that some of the basic properties of the normal universe will be reversed. In the case of an astronaut diving through the middle of a ring singularity, Gribbin explains,

the world is turned upside-down. The equations tell us that as you pass through the ring you enter a region of spacetime in which the product of your distance from the center of the ring and the force of gravity is *negative*. This might mean that gravity is behaving perfectly normally but you have entered a region of negative space in which it is possible to be, for example, "minus ten kilometers" away from the center of the hole. Even relativists [experts in general relativity] have trouble coming to terms with that possibility, so they usually interpret this negativity as meaning that *gravity* reverses as you pass through the ring, turning into a repulsive force that pushes you, instead of pulling. In the region of spacetime beyond the ring, the gravity of the black hole repels both matter and light away from itself.[48]

Problems with Wormholes

Although most physicists agree, at least in theory, that Gribbin's astronaut could enter and experience the strange effects of hyperspace inside the black hole, they caution that it is by no means certain that he or she could do so safely. First, they warn, there are serious dangers lurking outside the event horizon. Even before entering the black hole, the astronaut would have to find some way of surviving the extreme tidal forces and searing radiation in the spinning accretion disk.

For the sake of argument, however, assume that the astronaut manages to invent special shielding to protect against these lethal effects. And he or she makes it across the event horizon and into the black hole in one piece. From that point on, it is far from certain that the astronaut will be able to make it back to his or her starting point in space and time. Astronomer Sagan addresses this problem in *Contact:*

> As measured from Earth, it takes an infinite amount of time for us to pass through a black hole, and we could never, never return to Earth. . . . A Kerr-type tunnel can lead to grotesque causality violations [a breakdown of normal cause and effect]. With a modest change of trajectory [its path] inside the tunnel, one could emerge from the other end as early in the history of the universe as you might like—a picosecond [a small fraction of a second] after the Big Bang, for example. That would be a very disorderly universe.[49]

Still another challenge for the astronaut to overcome is the instability of the wormhole gateway and tunnel. A wormhole in a Kerr black hole might well remain open a good deal longer than the extremely short-lived version in a Schwarzschild black hole. However, a Kerr wormhole would still be highly fragile. Even the rather small gravitational effects created by the astronaut and his ship entering the tunnel might be enough to cause its collapse, which would simply crush the ship out of existence. According to Sagan:

> There is an interior tunnel in the exact Kerr solution of the Einstein field equations, but it's unstable. The slightest perturbation would seal it off and convert the tunnel into a physical singularity through which nothing can pass. I have tried to imagine a superior civilization that would control the internal structure of a collapsing star to keep the interior tunnel stable.

The Matricide Paradox

In his acclaimed book *Black Holes and Time Warps*, noted physicist Kip Thorne describes the phenomenon called the matricide paradox this way: "If I have a time machine . . . I should be able to use it to go back in time and kill my mother before I was conceived, thereby preventing myself from being born and killing my mother." Obviously, the paradox lies in the fact that the murder appears to stop itself from happening.

Thorne credits Joe Polchinski, a physicist at the University of Texas in Austin, with supplying the following scientific description of how the paradox might work:

> Take a wormhole that has been made into a time machine, and place its two mouths [each located at a black hole] at rest near each other out in interplanetary space. Then, if a billiard ball is launched toward the right mouth . . . with an appropriate initial velocity, the ball will enter the right mouth, travel backward in time, and fly out of the left mouth before it entered the right . . . and it will then hit its younger self, thereby preventing itself from ever entering the right mouth and hitting itself.

This is very difficult. The civilization would have to monitor and stabilize the tunnel forever. It would be especially difficult with something as large as [a spacecraft] falling through.[50]

The Need for Exotic Matter

This tendency of wormholes to collapse easily seems at first glance to rule out using such tunnels as gateways to other places and times. And this is the problem that Thorne, Morris, and Yurtsever faced when they began tinkering with the mathematics of black holes at Sagan's request. They were able to overcome the problem because they used a fresh approach. Instead of treating wormholes as hypothetical objects and trying to predict how they would work if they did exist, they began with the assumption that a stable, traversable wormhole *could* exist. They described the likely geometry of such an entity; and finally, they applied the principles of general relativity to predict what kind of matter would be needed to keep it open and stable.

In the film version of Carl Sagan's Contact, *astronaut Ellie Arroway prepares to enter hyperspace in a specially designed craft.*

The result was seen as a major breakthrough in theoretical physics. The Caltech team's equations showed that some kind of matter would be needed to exert the pressures required to keep the wormhole stable and open long enough for travelers to pass through. But ordinary matter does not exert enough pressure to do the job. Instead, some kind of *extra*ordinary matter would be needed. Thorne called it exotic matter, or material, about which he later wrote:

> I learned from the Einstein field equation, that, in order to gravitationally . . . push the wormhole's walls apart, *the exotic material threading the wormhole must have a negative energy density* [a state in which the material exerts no internal pressure, as material in the normal universe does]. . . . Because almost all forms of matter that we humans have ever encountered have positive average energy densities in *everyone's* reference frame, physicists have long suspected that exotic material cannot exist. . . . Then in 1974, came a great surprise. [Stephen] Hawking [determined] that *vacuum fluctuations* [random gravitational effects] *near a hole's* [event] *horizon are exotic.* . . . The horizon distorts the vacuum fluctuations away from the shapes they would have on Earth and by this distortion it makes their average energy density negative, that is, it makes them exotic.[51]

Although exotic matter has not been proven categorically to exist, a number of scientists think that measurable quantities of it may have drifted through the early universe. Perhaps, they say, small amounts of it still exist here and there in the present universe. Possibly, an advanced race of beings could find a way to manufacture exotic matter out of ordinary matter.

Time Tunnels and Primordial Bubbles

If exotic matter does exist naturally or else can be manufactured, the problem of keeping a wormhole open and stable would be solved. And barring any other unforeseen impediments, it would be possible to travel through such a cosmic tunnel. But why would someone embark on such a journey? Assuming they manage to develop the advanced technology required to stabilize and manipulate wormholes, why would humans or other intelligent beings choose travel in hyperspace over travel in ordinary space?

First, the math suggests that wormholes might create shortcuts to distant locations. In other words, if it takes a thousand years for a fast-moving spaceship to reach a faraway planetary system, manipulating a wormhole in just the right manner might allow the ship to make the trip in a much shorter amount of time. Scientists often point to the analogy of a watermelon, the outer surface of which represents normal space. An ant walking on the watermelon represents a spacecraft on a long journey to a distant location on the opposite side of the watermelon. Even when moving as fast as it can, the ant requires three full minutes to complete the trip. Just before setting out, however, the creature sees a nearby hole, the mouth of a tunnel that appears to go straight into the heart of the watermelon. The ant thinks twice about entering the hole because it seems to lead into an unknown region very different from the familiar realm of the surface. But it takes a chance and crawls down the hole. Following the tunnel, the ant travels straight through the center of the watermelon and climbs out of another hole on the opposite side, right beside its destination. The route it chose is shorter and more direct than the one on the surface, so the trip took only a minute instead of three.

In a similar manner, people in spaceships might someday take advantage of wormholes to reach faraway locations faster. If so, they will also travel through time. Just as time slows down for objects and people traveling near the speed of light in normal space, time will behave strangely and change-ably inside a black hole or in hyperspace. To an astronaut floating inside a black hole (if it is actually possible to do so), time would seem to pass quite normally. But from his or her point of view, the universe outside the event horizon would appear to move abnormally fast. The astronaut might remain in hyperspace for a week and then exit the wormhole to find that the world he or she left had aged ten thousand years.

Another possibility is that some wormholes might lead not to other parts of the known universe, but instead to unseen alternate universes. No direct evidence for such places has yet been found. But some scientists have suggested that the violent explosion

An artist captures a dramatic vision of the M87 galaxy, with immense jets produced by a central black hole of 5 billion solar masses.

of the Big Bang could conceivably have created "bubbles," shells encasing distorted regions of space and time separate from and completely invisible to ordinary space and time. There is no guarantee that the known laws of physics would be the same inside these bubble universes. So any humans who entered such a place via a wormhole might die instantly, or at least find themselves in an unimaginably bizarre and hostile environment.

Invoking the image of the Big Bang suggests one final, mind-bending concept involving black holes. As near as scientists can tell, that tremendous primeval explosion expanded outward from a single, infinitely small point in spacetime, a point exactly like the theoretical singularity of a black hole. Perhaps the known universe emerged from a massive superdense object. And the atoms making up our bodies, Earth, the stars, and everything else we can see coalesced from the compact, swirling energies buried deep inside the guts of the greatest of all cosmic monsters. As Begelman and Rees put it:

> Hidden from view inside their "horizons," [black holes] hold secrets that transcend the physics we understand. The central "singularity" involves the same physics that occurred at the initial instants of the Big Bang and will recur again if the universe recollapses. When we really understand black holes, we will understand the origin of the universe itself.[52]

Notes

Introduction: Facing the Ultimate Unknowable

1. Kip S. Thorne, *Black Holes and Time Warps: Einstein's Outrageous Legacy*. New York: W.W. Norton, 1994, p. 23.
2. Thorne, *Black Holes and Time Warps*, p. 23.
3. John Taylor, *Black Holes: The End of the Universe?* London: Souvenir, 1998, p. 1.
4. Mitchell Begelman and Martin Rees, *Gravity's Fatal Attraction: Black Holes in the Universe*. New York: W.H. Freeman, 1995, p. 19.
5. Begelman and Rees, *Gravity's Fatal Attraction*, pp. 19–21.

Chapter 1: Gravity and Early Predictions of Black Holes

6. Thomas T. Arny, *Explorations: An Introduction to Astronomy*. New York: McGraw-Hill, 2001, p. 405.
7. John Gribbin, *In Search of the Edge of Time: Black Holes, White Holes, and Wormholes*. New York: Penguin, 1999, p. 9.
8. Isaac Asimov, *The Collapsing Universe*, 1977; reprint, New York: Walker, 1989, pp. 44, 46.
9. John Michell, "On the Means of Discovering the Distance, Magnitude, etc., of the Fixed Stars," *Philosophical Transaction of the Royal Society of London*, vol. 74, 1784, p. 35.
10. Quoted in Gribbin, *In Search of the Edge of Time*, p. 21.
11. Arny, *Explorations*, p. 404.
12. Asimov, *Collapsing Universe*, p. 94.
13. John A. Wheeler, *A Journey into Gravity and Spacetime*. New York: W.H. Freeman, 1990, p. 3.

Chapter 2: Dying Stars and the Formation of Black Holes

14. Asimov, *Collapsing Universe*, pp. 198–99.
15. Asimov, *Collapsing Universe*, p. 200.
16. Begelman and Rees, *Gravity's Fatal Attraction*, p. 15.
17. Begelman and Rees, *Gravity's Fatal Attraction*, p. 15.

18. Asimov, *Collapsing Universe*, p. 84.
19. Begelman and Rees, *Gravity's Fatal Attraction*, p. 32.
20. Herbert Friedman, *The Astronomer's Universe: Stars, Galaxies, and Cosmos*. New York: W.W. Norton, 1998, p. 195.
21. Gribbin, *In Search of the Edge of Time*, p. 74.

Chapter 3: Properties and Potential Uses of Black Holes
22. Gribbin, *In Search of the Edge of Time*, p. 130.
23. Arny, *Explorations*, p. 70.
24. Asimov, *Collapsing Universe*, p. 217.
25. Thorne, *Black Holes and Time Warps*, p. 291.
26. Thorne, *Black Holes and Time Warps*, pp. 349–50.
27. Gribbin, *In Search of the Edge of Time*, p. 149.
28. Taylor, *Black Holes*, p. 87.
29. Asimov, *Collapsing Universe*, p. 205.

Chapter 4: Detecting Black Holes Through Indirect Means
30. Friedman, *Astronomer's Universe*, p. 80.
31. Gribbin, *In Search of the Edge of Time*, p. 106.
32. Friedman, *Astronomer's Universe*, p. 219.
33. Begelman and Rees, *Gravity's Fatal Attraction*, p. 71.
34. William Keel, "Quasars Explained," *Astronomy*, February 2003, p. 37.
35. Mark A. Garlick, "Quasars Next Door," *Astronomy*, July 2001, pp. 35–36.

Chapter 5: Giant Black Holes and the Fate of the Universe
36. Asimov, *Collapsing Universe*, p. 190.
37. Quoted in Vanessa Thomas, "Dark Heart of a Globular," *Astronomy*, January 2003, p. 32.
38. Robert Zimmerman, "Heart of Darkness," *Astronomy*, October 2001, pp. 43–44.
39. Zimmerman, "Heart of Darkness," p. 46.
40. Keel, "Quasars Explained," p. 40.
41. Keel, "Quasars Explained," p. 40.
42. Steve Nadis, "Here, There, and Everywhere?" *Astronomy*, February 2001, p. 34.
43. Asimov, *Collapsing Universe*, pp. 191–92.
44. Quoted in Nadis, "Here, There, and Everywhere?" p. 37.

45. Taylor, *Black Holes*, p. 182.

Chapter 6: Can Black Holes Be Used as Cosmic Gateways?

46. Thorne, *Black Holes and Time Warps*, p. 490.
47. Gribbin, *In Search of the Edge of Time*, p. 152.
48. Gribbin, *In Search of the Edge of Time*, p. 163.
49. Carl Sagan, *Contact*. New York: Simon and Schuster, 1985, pp. 347–48.
50. Sagan, *Contact*, p. 347.
51. Thorne, *Black Holes and Time Warps*, pp. 488, 490–92.
52. Begelman and Rees, *Gravity's Fatal Attraction*, p. 235.

Glossary

accretion disk: A flattened disk of matter rotating around an object with powerful gravity, such as a neutron star or black hole.

black hole: A superdense object with gravity so strong that not even light can escape it.

curved space: The concept, first advanced by German scientist Albert Einstein, that space has an invisible fabric that bends when objects with mass move across it.

dense: Highly compact.

escape velocity: The speed that a body needs to travel to escape the gravity of another body.

event horizon: The point of no return near a black hole. Any matter that crosses the event horizon disappears forever into the black hole.

exotic matter: A hypothetical kind of matter possessing the strength to hold open and stabilize a wormhole.

galactic black hole: A supermassive black hole lying at the center of a galaxy.

galaxy: A gigantic group of stars held together by their mutual gravities. Our galaxy is called the Milky Way.

gamma-ray burst (GRB): A powerful outburst of gamma rays originating from beyond our solar system.

gravity: A force exerted by an object that attracts other objects. The pull of Earth's gravity keeps rocks, people, and houses from floating away into space and holds the Moon in its orbit around Earth.

gravity well: A depression in the fabric of space created by the mass of an object The more massive the object, the deeper the well.

hyperspace: A hypothetical region lying outside of and that is invisible to ordinary space.

Kerr black hole: A spinning black hole.

light-year: The distance that light travels in a year, or about 6 trillion miles.

mass: The measurable matter making up an object.

neutron star: A superdense object made up almost entirely of neutrons, which forms from the collapse of a large star.

pulsar: A cosmic object that seems to emit energy in rapid pulses; astronomers have shown that pulsars are swiftly rotating neutron stars.

quasar: An extremely powerful energy source located at the center of a distant galaxy; astronomers now believe that quasars are caused by galactic black holes.

red giant: A stage of stellar evolution in which excess heat produced in a star's core causes it to swell to huge proportions; as it swells, its outer layers cool enough to make them turn from yellow to red.

Schwarzschild black hole: A theoretical nonspinning black hole.

Schwarzschild radius: The distance from a black hole's center point, or singularity, to its event horizon.

singularity: The pointlike center of a black hole.

solar mass: The mass of the Sun; scientists often measure the size of black holes, neutron stars, and even ordinary stars in solar masses.

solar system: The Sun and all the planets, moons, asteroids, and other objects held by the Sun's gravity.

stellar: Having to do with stars.

stellar collapse: A violent event in which gravity causes a star to collapse inward on itself, squashing most of its material into a small, very dense object.

supernova: A tremendous explosion that occurs during the gravitational collapse of a large star. The gases and other debris sent flying by the explosion are called the supernova remnant.

tidal effect: An intense gravitational attraction.

time dilation: A phenomenon in which the time frame of matter traveling at near-light speeds seems to slow down in comparison with the time frame of matter moving at normal speeds.

universe: The sum total of all the space and matter known to exist.

white dwarf: A superdense object that forms from the collapse of an average-sized star.

wormhole: A theoretical invisible tunnel connecting a black hole to another spot in the universe.

X-ray binary: A double star system in which one star collapses into a very dense object, usually a white dwarf, neutron star, or black hole.

For Further Reading

Books

Alex Barret and Stuart Clark, *Secret Worlds: Black Holes*. London: Dorling Kindersley, 2002. An up-to-date overview of the subject with many colorful illustrations.

Heather Couper and Nigel Henbest, *Black Holes*. London: Dorling Kindersley, 1996. A handsomely illustrated book that explains the basic concepts surrounding black holes in easy terms for young people. Highly recommended.

Nigel Henbest, *DK Space Encyclopedia*. London: Dorling Kindersley, 1999. This beautifully mounted and critically acclaimed book is the best general source available for grade school readers about the wonders of space. Older readers will find it useful, too.

Patrick Moore, *Astronomy Encyclopedia*. New York: Oxford University Press, 2002. This handsomely illustrated book contains hundreds of short articles about all aspects of the stars, planets, and other celestial bodies, including white dwarfs, neutron stars, and black holes.

Chris Oxlade, *The Mystery of Black Holes*. Crystal Lake, IL: Heineman Library, 1999. One of the better books about black holes written for young readers.

Paul P. Sipiera, *Black Holes*. Danbury, CT: Childrens Press, 1997. A commendable general overview of the subject with some attractive illustrations.

Internet Sources

"Black Holes," Cambridge Relativity, 1996. www.damtp.cam.ac.uk. A general overview of black holes, with many stunning color photos and diagrams.

"NASA Spacelink," NASA. http://spacelink.nasa.gov. This leads to an excellent site about black holes, with numerous links to other sites explaining different aspects of the subject. Highly recommended.

Robert Nemiroff, "Virtual Trips to Black Holes and Neutron Stars," NASA. http://antwrp.gsfc.nasa.gov. A series of excellent, accurate graphics allow viewers to approach, circle, and at times even land on black holes and neutron stars. Also has links to pages with background information.

Major Works Consulted

Isaac Asimov, *The Collapsing Universe.* 1977. Reprint, New York: Walker, 1989. Published before some of the major discoveries confirming many aspects of black holes, this volume is now somewhat dated. However, thanks to Asimov's remarkable skills in research and explaining difficult scientific concepts in simple ways, this remains one of the best general overviews of black holes, white dwarfs, and neutron stars. Highly recommended, especially for novices in the subject.

Mitchell Begelman and Martin Rees, *Gravity's Fatal Attraction: Black Holes in the Universe.* New York: W.H. Freeman, 1995. An excellent, highly informative discussion of black holes, including related phenomena such as stellar evolution and collapses, supernovas, white dwarfs, neutron stars, and quasars.

John Gribbin, *In Search of the Edge of Time: Black Holes, White Holes, and Wormholes.* New York: Penguin, 1999. A well-written, well-informed investigation of some of the more bizarre astronomical phenomena, along with the story of how scientists discovered them. Highly recommended. (This book was first released in the United States as *Unveiling the Edge of Time.*)

Clifford A. Pickover, *Black Holes: A Traveler's Guide.* New York: John Wiley, 1998. Very well written, this book makes the more difficult concepts about black holes and curved space very understandable and accessible. A clever and helpful added feature is a short dialogue between the author and an alien at the end of each chapter, foreshadowing the information that will come in the next chapter.

Edwin F. Taylor and John A. Wheeler, *Black Holes: Introduction to General Relativity.* San Francisco: Benjamin Cummings, 2000. This is an excellent study of the subject, but since it is on the scholarly side, it requires that the reader possess a fairly high proficiency in math.

John Taylor, *Black Holes: The End of the Universe?* London: Souvenir, 1998. A thought-provoking journey into aspects of black holes and what Taylor calls the "black hole universe" that most books on the subject do not attempt to address, including the ultimate fate of humanity—to be absorbed into and destroyed by a black hole, and the possibility that souls, if they exist, might be able to survive the big crunch. Intriguing.

Kip S. Thorne, *Black Holes and Time Warps: Einstein's Outrageous Legacy.* New York: W.W. Norton, 1994. Arguably the best book written so far about black holes and related phenomena. Combines history, science, and first-rate scholarship in an almost definitive statement about the effects of extreme gravity on the workings of space and time. Highly recommended.

Clifford Will, *Was Einstein Right?* New York: Basic Books, 1993. This award-winning book is a wonderful, easy-to-read exploration of Einstein's theory of relativity, which takes into account the concept of black holes. Highly recommended for those interested in curved space and black holes, or for anyone who enjoys reading about science.

Additional Works Consulted

Books

Thomas T. Arny, *Explorations: An Introduction to Astronomy.* New York: McGraw-Hill, 2001.

Herbert Friedman, *The Astronomer's Universe: Stars, Galaxies, and Cosmos.* New York: W.W. Norton, 1998.

George Gamow, *The Creation of the Universe.* New York: Viking, 1961.

Norman K. Glendenning, *Compact Stars: Nuclear Physics, Particle Physics, and General Relativity.* Heidelberg, Germany: Springer Verlag, 2000.

Stephen Hawking, *Black Holes and Baby Universes and Other Essays.* New York: Bantam, 1994.

———, *A Brief History of Time.* New York: Bantam, 1998.

Robert M. Hazen and James Trefil, *Science Matters: Achieving Scientific Literacy.* New York: Doubleday, 1991.

Robert Jastrow, *Red Giants and White Dwarfs.* New York: W.W. Norton, 1990.

Michio Kaku, *Hyperspace: A Scientific Odyssey Through Parallel Universes, Time Warps, and the 10th Dimension.* New York: Anchor, 1995.

William C. Keel, *The Road to Galaxy Formation.* New York: Praxis, 2002.

Lawrence M. Krauss, *The Physics of Star Trek.* New York: HarperCollins, 1995.

Carl Sagan, *Contact.* New York: Simon and Schuster, 1985.

Paul Strathern, *Hawking and Black Holes.* New York: Anchor, 1997.

R.M. Wald, *Space, Time, and Gravity: The Story of the Big Bang and Black Holes*. Chicago: University of Chicago Press, 1992.

John A. Wheeler, *A Journey into Gravity and Spacetime*. New York: W.H. Freeman, 1990.

Periodicals

Albert Einstein and Nathan Rosen, "The Particle Problem in the General Theory of Relativity," *Physics Review*, vol. 48, 1935.

Andrew Fazekas, "Mid-Size Black Holes," *Astronomy*, July 2003.

Mark A. Garlick, "Quasars Next Door," *Astronomy*, July 2001.

S.S. Hall, "The Man Who Invented Time Travel: The Astounding World of Kip Thorne," *California*, October 1989.

Stephen W. Hawking, "Black Hole Explosions?" *Nature*, vol. 248, 1974.

———, "Black Holes in General Relativity," *Communications in Mathematical Physics*, vol. 25, 1972.

Ray Jayawardana, "Beyond Black," *Astronomy*, June 2002.

William Keel, "Quasars Explained," *Astronomy*, February 2003.

Jean-Pierre Lasota, "Unmasking Black Holes," *Scientific American*, May 1999.

John Michell, "On the Means of Discovering the Distance, Magnitude, etc., of the Fixed Stars," *Philosophical Transaction of the Royal Society of London*, vol. 74, 1784.

Paul Morledge, "Black Hole Bites More Than It Can Chew," *Astronomy*, February 2002.

———, "New Sources of Gamma Bursts," *Astronomy*, June 2002.

Steve Nadis, "Here, There, and Everywhere?" *Astronomy*, February 2001.

William Schomaker, "Black Hole Goes for a Spin," *Astronomy*, August 2001.

————, "Of Starbursts and Black Holes," *Astronomy*, September 2001.

Michael Shara, "When Stars Collide," *Scientific American*, November 2002.

Richard Talcott, "Jets from a Black Hole," *Astronomy*, January 2003.

————, "Seeing a Black Hole's Edge," *Astronomy*, October 2001.

————, "Seeing an Invisible Horizon," *Astronomy*, May 2001.

Max Tegmark, "Parallel Universes," *Scientific American*, May 2003.

Vanessa Thomas, "Dark Heart of a Globular," *Astronomy*, January 2003.

————, "Life-Giving Black Holes," *Astronomy*, July 2003.

————, "When Black Holes Collide," *Astronomy*, November 2002.

Kip S. Thorne, "The Search for Black Holes," *Scientific American*, vol. 231, 1974.

Robert Zimmerman, "Heart of Darkness," *Astronomy*, October 2001.

Internet Sources

Fredrik Berndtson et al., "Wormholes and Time Machines," n.d., *Chalmers Physics*. www.dd.chalmers.se.

"Chandra Sees Wealth of Black Holes in Star-Forming Galaxies," July 5, 2001, Harvard-Smithsonian Center for Astrophysics. http://chandra.harvard.edu.

"A Galaxy Center Mystery," February 21, 2002, NASA. http://science.nasa.gov.

Michio Kaku, "Black Holes, Wormholes, and the 10th Dimension," n.d., *Cosmology Today*. www.flash.net.

"A New Class of Black Holes," April 13, 1999, NASA. http://science.nasa.gov.

"New Evidence for Black Holes," January 12, 2001, NASA. http://science.nasa.gov.

Index

Picture Credits

Cover image: © Reuters NewMedia Inc./CORBIS
© Lucien Aigner/CORBIS, 21
© Julian Baum/Photo Researchers, Inc., 68, 91
© John Foster/Photo Researchers, Inc., 8
© David A. Hardy/Photo Researchers, Inc., 33, 47, 59
© JISAS/Lockheed/Photo Researchers, Inc., 55
Chris Jouan, 17, 22, 30, 44, 50, 60, 85
© Douglas Kirkland/CORBIS, 41
© Lawrence Livermore National Laboratory/Photo Researchers, Inc., 11
Library of Congress, 14
© Dr. Jean Lorre/Photo Researchers, Inc., 77
NASA/CXC/MIT/F.K. Baganoff, et al., 75
NASA/CXC/NGST, 56
NASA/CXC/A. Siemiginowska (CfA)/J. Bechtold (U. Arizona), 65
NASA, A. Fruchter and the ERO Team, STScI, ST-ECF, 24
NASA, The Hubble Heritage Team, STScI, AURA, 71
© NASA/Photo Researchers, Inc., 36
© NOAO/AURA/NSF/Photo Researchers, Inc., 70
Photofest, 82, 88
© Science Photo Library/Photo Researchers, Inc., 27
© Space Telescope Science Institute/NASA/Photo Researchers, Inc., 13, 62

About the Author

In addition to his acclaimed volumes on ancient civilizations, historian Don Nardo has published several studies of modern scientific discoveries and phenomena. Among these are *Lasers, Comets and Asteroids, Extraterrestrial Life, The Extinction of the Dinosaurs, Cloning*, volumes about Pluto, Neptune, the asteroids, and the Moon, and a biography of the noted scientist Charles Darwin. Mr. Nardo lives with his wife, Christine, in Massachusetts.